THE CAREERS OF BUSINESS MANAGERS IN EAST ASIA

THE CAREERS OF
BUSINESS MANAGERS
IN EAST ASIA

Edited by
Cherlyn Skromme Granrose

QUORUM BOOKS
Westport, Connecticut • London

Copyright Acknowledgements

Chapters 2, 3, 4, 5, and 6 of this volume are revised versions of the articles appearing in a special issue of the *Journal of Asian Business*, Volume 11, Number 3, 1995. Each of these chapters is reprinted with the permission of the Association for Asian Studies Inc.

Table 1.1 is reprinted from *The boundaryless career: A new employment principle for a new organizational era*, edited by Michael B. Arthur and D. M. Rousseau. Copyright © 1996 by Michael B. Arthur et al. Used by permission of Oxford University Press Inc.

Library of Congress Cataloging-in-Publication Data

The careers of business managers in East Asia / edited by Cherlyn
   Skromme Granrose.
      p.   cm.
   Includes bibliographical references and index.
   ISBN 1–56720–101–6 (alk. paper)
     1. Executives—East Asia—Case studies. 2. Management—East Asia—
Case studies. I. Granrose, Cherlyn S.
HD38.25.E18C37   1997
331.7'616584'0095—dc21   97–1703

British Library Cataloguing in Publication Data is available.

Library of Congress Catalog Card Number: 97–1703
ISBN: 1–56720–101–6

First published in 1997

Quorum Books, 88 Post Road West, Westport, CT 06881
An imprint of Greenwood Publishing Group, Inc.

Printed in the United States of America

The paper used in this book complies with the
Permanent Paper Standard issued by the National
Information Standards Organization (Z39.48–1984).

10 9 8 7 6 5 4 3 2 1

Contents

Tables and Figures

TABLES

FIGURES

Preface

The idea for this volume started at an Academy of Management Careers pre-conference workshop, when I heard scholars from Singapore and India declare that current U.S. career theory really does not apply to careers in their nations. Those comments and the response of Michael B. Arthur, who was one of the scholars convening the workshop, stimulated me to learn about cross-cultural research in general and Asian cultures in particular. In response to this experience, I obtained a Fulbright Research Fellowship to study careers of Asian managers. I am deeply indebted to the Fulbright Scholars program for its financial support and in particular to David Adams, Fulbright senior program officer for East Asia, for his support and mentoring as I was beginning my work in Singapore. In addition to support from the Fulbright program, I appreciate the sabbatical support I received from Temple University and the financial assistance I received from the Temple University Center for East Asian Studies to return to Asia to continue this project.

As I was collecting data from Asian employees of U.S. firms, I asked Asian scholars in each country to collect data on Asian managers employed in domestic firms in the same industries. This volume is the primary result of that collaboration. In addition to the authors of individual chapters appearing in this volume, several scholars, especially Samuel Aryee, Mary Lou Onglatco, and Irene Chew, at the National University of Singapore were helpful in developing a questionnaire suitable for an Asian context. Research in each location was supported by the scholars' university, and additional funding was obtained from the Taiwanese government for data gathered in that country.

Several of the chapters appeared in slightly different form in a special issue of the *Journal of Asian Business*, and I am grateful to Linda Lim, Jason Eyster, and Helen White for their cooperation and the suggestions they contributed to this volume. I also value the feedback and editorial advice of Stuart Oskamp and several anonymous journal reviewers.

I received invaluable assistance from my research assistant Madan Anavarjula, who coded data from many slightly different national versions of the questionnaire, and B. J. Reich and Huyen Cao, who turned many different fonts and word processing programs into one manuscript. These individuals bore the brunt of the most tedious steps of integrating specific information from many different cultures into a single whole. Thank you.

Introduction

Cherlyn Skromme Granrose

Managers of human resources in international firms have experienced numerous problems when they attempt to export domestic policies into other nations. International executives find that managers in different locations differ in goals and aspirations, as well as in the strategies, plans, and systems they use to achieve these goals. The cultural and national differences between employee expectations and firm policies often result in dissatisfied employees, unexpected productivity difficulties, and higher than desired rates of turnover.

When practitioners seek scholarly advice to solve the problems that arise from these differences, they are confronted with theory and data that describe primarily European or American experiences. While international human resources strategy is beginning to suggest policy alternatives, and cross-cultural psychology has long explored individual differences in all parts of the globe, specific information about the career desires, plans, and expectations of managers outside of Europe and North America has remained scarce. This volume seeks to fill one gap in our knowledge by providing career information about managers in three key Asian business locations: Taiwan, Hong Kong, and Japan. Subsequent work from the project upon which this book is based will provide similar information about other Asian locations.

Chapter 1, by Michael B. Arthur, provides a summary of past Euro-American career research highlights and, using these themes as lenses focused on the world, introduces questions we must understand if we want to extend our knowledge into Asia. In Chapter 2, Cherlyn Skromme

Granrose proposes a theoretical framework to analyze careers at the national, organizational, and individual level. This framework served as the guidelines for deciding what kinds of data to gather in the research reported in the rest of the volume.

Chapter 3 on Hong Kong managers' careers (Irene Hau-Siu Chow), Chapter 4 on Taiwanese managers' careers (Tai-Kuang Peng) and Chapter 5 on Japanese managers' careers (Masao Baba, Cherlyn Skromme Granrose, and Allan Bird) use this framework to describe in quantitative and qualitative terms the career goals, career tactics, and career satisfaction of individual managers as well as the domestic organizational human resources practices common to each country.

In order to gather comparable data from each country, a similar group of core questions was asked in each location, with additional changes made to more adequately describe individual country differences. Copies of the questionnaire used for line managers can be found in Appendix A, and the interview protocol for human resources managers is located in Appendix B.

Data were collected in English from employees of U.S. firms and in Chinese and Japanese from employees of home country firms. One or more manufacturing firms and one or more service firms in each country, as well as government-related organizations in Taiwan and Hong Kong, provided the research sites. This research does not address careers of managers in small businesses common to these locations. Each chapter includes employees working for U.S. and for home country companies. Differences between employees in different industries or between employees of U.S. and home firms are described as they occur.

Since major social and business practice changes are occurring in each of these countries as their economies change, a description of the status of the country at the time of reporting is included in each chapter. These reports of career practices and beliefs in a particular economic context may serve as a baseline against which to evaluate rapid changes in the future.

Chapter 6 (Rey-Yeh Lin) uses data from each of the samples reported in the preceding chapters, as well as data from managers employed by U.S. firms in Singapore to compare career goals and career tactics across cultures. The analysis represents an initial comparison of key concepts that begins to clarify commonalities and differences in these settings.

Although these data cannot begin to adequately describe all the career patterns occurring in each country, they do offer initial evidence of issues which human resources managers may want to consider as they develop policies for managers from Japan, Hong Kong, and Taiwan. In addition, scholars may be able to use the information presented here to rethink their career theory to include concepts and relationships generalizable beyond North America and Europe.

CHAPTER ONE

Exploring Asian Careers: Looking at the East through the Lenses of the West

Michael B. Arthur

> From 1945 to 1995, half a century, Asia went from rags to riches. It reduced the incidence of poverty from 400 million to 180 million, while its population grew by 400 million in the same period. The World Bank has pronounced that nowhere and at no time in human history has humanity achieved such economic progress, and concluded that the East Asia story is an economic miracle. My studies in Asia convince me of that miracle yes; but it has not been purely economics. The story of the New Asia is a story of the miracle of the human spirit, driven by an awakening to one's own potential and propelled by the power of determination, and of the progress achieved by toil and sacrifice.
>
> John Naisbitt, *Megatrends Asia,* 1995

John Naisbitt's "miracle of the human spirit" may be equally described as a miracle of Asian careers, for it is through peoples' careers—that is, their work behaviors over time—that Asian economies have aroused peoples' "own potential," propelled "the power of determination," and rewarded "toil and sacrifice." If Naisbitt is right, the study of Asian careers offers rich returns.

However, if Naisbitt *is* right, there is much that we previously got wrong. For example, the uninitiated reader might presume that Naisbitt's book is an extension of the "Japanese miracle" argument that so fascinated the West until the early 1990s. However, Naisbitt cites Japan's "long downward slide," where the "lifetime employment" economy has failed and overregulation and underwork are debilitating national handicaps. Naisbitt worries that the political West "continues to be the prisoner of the vocabulary and concepts of the nation-state, Cold War period," shifting its obsession from Japan to China. Meanwhile, "Governments do not create the world's added value. People do." We can add that people create value through their careers, and thus a closer understanding of those careers is vital.

Let us explore how such a closer understanding can be pursued. The problem for the Western observer may be expressed in two parts. First, what are—to use Naisbitt's terms—the vocabulary and concepts we bring to our studies of Asian careers? Second, how do our data respond to or influence the vocabulary and concepts that we employ? In the sections that follow, I will explore these questions through two sets of lenses. The first set, still dominant in career studies today, employs what Naisbitt labels the "old paradigm" of nation-state, or "industrial state," logic. The second set, still in the early stage of being crafted, employs a more open or "boundaryless" logic to both careers and their host economies.

CAREER STUDIES THROUGH ESTABLISHED LENSES

Western interest in the concept of career as a serious focus of employment research traces back to the mid-1970s at the Massachusetts Institute of Technology (MIT) and to a group of four exceptional scholars still active today. This "MIT quartet"—psychologist Douglas (Tim) Hall who completed his Ph.D. at MIT, social psychologist Lotte Bailyn, sociologist John Van Maanen, and industrial psychologist Edgar Schein—produced three landmark books that many still rely on (Hall, 1976; Van Maanen, 1977; Schein, 1978). They also made four essential contributions to subsequent career studies.

The first contribution was to affirm a definition of career—the sequence of a person's work experiences over time—that applies to all workers and all sequences of work roles. This definition, drawn in turn from both the University of Chicago perspective on sociology (Hughes, 1958) and the Columbia University perspective of educational psychology (Super, 1957), insists that the concept of career is applicable to all people and all forms of organization. The second contribution was to insist that the time dimension be recognized as a key mediator of individual–organizational relationships, in contrast to other efforts such as job satisfaction or job design. The third contribution, one which could uniquely come from management research, was to establish the career as a focus for interdisciplinary study. Psychology, sociology, anthropology, political science, and economics could all be harnessed for their contributions to our composite understanding of how careers unfold.

The fourth contribution was to see the career from both subjective and objective perspectives. The subjective refers generally to the individual's own interpretation of his or her career situation. The objective refers to institutional—organizational or societal—interpretations of the same career situation. This duality of perspectives distinguishes career studies from other social sciences, where subjective and objective views are often represented as opposite ends of the same continuum (e.g., Burrell & Morgan, 1979). Taken together, the four contributions of the MIT quartet define a unique place for career studies in the management research agenda.

There are two other legacies of this groundbreaking work in career studies that we should note. The first legacy can be spotted in the titles of the foundational texts. *Careers in Organizations* (Hall, 1976), *Organizational Careers* (Van Maanen, 1977) and (Schein's subtitle) *Matching Individual and Organizational Needs* (Schein, 1978) all conveyed the assumption that careers should be studied within the boundaries of a single organization. (Despite the book's main theme and title, Hall's work does conclude with the idea of the "protean career described explicitly as not what happens to the person in any one organization" [Hall, 1976, p. 201]). The assumption of careers in one organization was consistent with the broader field of organizational behavior and with parallel applied career development, organization development, and quality of work life initiatives to improve the lot of the working person. We assumed an industrial state populated by large entrenched organizations. Naisbitt's argument in the introduction to this chapter is that we still assume such a state.

A further legacy can be identified in a subsequent book titled *Managing Career Systems* (Sonnenfeld, 1984). The argument that career systems matter reasserted the MIT quartet's interest in organizational career contexts, and not just in individual *Self-Assessment and Career Development* (Kotter, Faux, & McArthur, 1978). However, the subtitle of the Sonnenfeld volume—*Channelling the Flow of Executive Careers*—narrowed the universal view of careers to a more limited executive or managerial and professional community. This narrowing contrasts once more with the opening quotation from Naisbitt, whose story of the New Asia celebrates everyone who works.

A final point to be made about the MIT initiative is its implication of environmental stability. The theorists' focus was on what happened inside rather than outside the boundary of the organization. In taking this focus, career studies was in step with multiple other factions of organizational inquiry and prone to neglect pressures of outside competition (witness certain special issues of major journals, such as those edited by Daft and Lewin (1993) and Prahalad and Hamel (1994) on new paradigms for organization and strategy). One notable exception to this assumption of environmental stability—and where career studies played a further leadership role—was in the arena of dual-career and work and family issues. In this arena, the fluctuating demands of raising children were depicted to require unstable career investments (e.g., Bailyn, 1978).

Established Lenses on the East: The Case of Japan

About the time the MIT quartet was establishing a new movement in the study of careers, Western interest was being drawn to the East, and in particular to the growing competitiveness of Japan. By the early 1980s, three best-selling books had been published: Pascale and Athos's (1981) *The Art of Japanese Management*, Ouchi's (1981) *Theory Z*, and Peters and Waterman's (1982) *In Search of Excellence*, each drawing inspiration from Japan's competitive success.

The Art of Japanese Management sought to paint a contrast between Japanese and U.S. management practices and is anchored in a comparison between large-firm examples of Matsushita and ITT. One message for career scholars was that individual needs should be subordinated to group needs, allowing for greater corporate investment in human resources development (p. 87). Despite this group orientation, in urging people to "accept ambiguity, uncertainty and imperfection as much more of a given" there was an underlying message that managerial careers were not so different from the West: "Very few professionals are content simply to compete in the race for corporate recognition. Most want to win or, at least, to place among those at the head of the pack" (p. 107). The book acknowledged the relevance of career reputation (p. 143), but only as it applied *inside* the employing organization. Closing discussion about great companies—all large companies—leaned heavily on IBM as an exemplar of lifetime employment.

Theory Z reaffirmed the general cultural messages from *The Art of Japanese Management* and extended the emphasis on large Japanese firms. Supposedly, the dominance of the old military–industrial *zaibatsu*, legally dissolved after World War II, prevailed (p. 19). Meanwhile, smaller satellite firms were described to "exist largely at the pleasure and the mercy of the major firms," and to "have little hope of ever growing into major competitors" (p. 21). No mention was made of the *kieretsu*, which, in contrast to the *zaibatsu* idea, acknowledges the degree of independence so-called satellite firms possess. There was an explicit message that careers involved "stable, lifetime employment" as "a reality for the [admittedly] male employees of major firms" (p. 22) and continuous learning through, for example, "a process of lifelong job rotation" that "holds true for all employees in many Japanese firms" (p. 28). Ouchi went on to applaud large American firms, among them General Motors, Ford, Chrysler, Hewlett Packard, Honeywell, and IBM, for their attempts to develop a

Type Z culture offering employees "a stable social setting in which to get their bearings and draw support to cope with and build the other parts of their lives" (p. 166).

In Search of Excellence drew on the same framework underlying *The Art of Japanese Management* but leaped straight to the task of identifying "excellence" within American corporations. The concept of career was left implicit, although "productivity through people" was a basic axiom of the excellence message. However, there were references to "liking to think of ourselves as winners" (p. 57), our "need for meaning" (p. 77), and "the need to control one's destiny," to which career scholars can relate and use as points of departure. Peters and Waterman then turned to emphasize simultaneous needs for "self-determination and security" (p. 80). The so-called excellent companies were supposed to deliver on both of these seemingly opposite motivations. Familiar, predominantly large, organizational examples—including Caterpillar, Digital, General Motors, Hewlett-Packard, and IBM—were cited as exemplary.

In sum, all three of these books emphasized the importance of large firms and lifelong employment within them. Also, although there was a shared message about the general importance of people, it was easy to draw from both *The Art of Japanese Management* and *In Search of Excellence* that it was the careers of senior managers, as shapers of culture, transformational leaders, and sponsors of quality circles, that mattered most. As we have seen, this managerial career emphasis was explicit in *Theory Z*. These managers clearly overlap with the MIT quartet's focus on intraorganizational, managerial, and professional career themes.

The Case for New Lenses

Assumptions about large unchanging firms, and of organizational careers within those firms, persist. So do assumptions of Japanese careers popularized a decade or more ago. Features in *Newsweek* (1996) and the *New York Times* (1996) bemoan the downsizing of America and embrace a return to more traditional career arrangements. A survey of Western research found that environmental stability, large firms, hierarchical careers, and an intrafirm focus continue to be assumed in three out of four studies about careers (Arthur and Rousseau, 1996, pp. 3–20). A broader sample of research into work and employment still emphasizes environmental stability, large firms, and traditional—largely static—job arrangements (see Table 1.1).

However, these assumptions increasingly are being challenged, not the least by fresh evidence from Asia. There is a strengthening belief that we can offer better career lenses to provide Naisbitt's "new paradigm" insight into the world of work (Naisbitt, 1995).

Table 1.1
Studies of Careers, Work, and Employment in Five Interdisciplinary Journals

	Research on Careers		Research on Work and Employment[a]
	1980-1989	1990-1994	1990-1994
Theme	Number %	Number %	Number %
Environmental stability[b]	43 93	43 74	71 67
Intrafirm focus	36 78	44 76	97 91[c]
Hierarchical assumptions[d]	35 76	47 81	70 66[e]
Size			
Large firms			
(> 500 employees)	21 46	21 36	42 40
Smaller firms			
(< 500 employees)	7 17	5 9	13 12
Mixed-size firms[f]	2 4	9 16	26 25
Occupational or industry			
sample	14 30	23 40	22 21
Experimental research	— —	— —	7 7
Total number of articles	46 100	58 100	106 100

Sources: Empirical research from the *Academy of Management Journal, Administrative Science Quarterly, Journal of Management, Journal of Management Studies,* and *Journal of Organizational* (formerly *Occupational*) *Behavior.*
a. Subsample of a sample of 150 articles—6 per year from each journal.
b. Presumed wherever environmental change was not signaled in the article.
c. Five additional articles could not be reasonably classified.
d. Includes career studies restricted to managerial and professional employees.
e. Twenty-six additional articles could not be reasonably classified.
f. Includes occasional best estimates from the data provided.

CAREER STUDIES THROUGH NEW LENSES

Although, as we have seen, much empirical work on careers has stayed within the confines of established views, certain recent authors have suggested a different approach. One way or another, they take issue with the picture of a stable, large-firm-dominated, intra-organizational world of managers and professionals, on which much empirical work has been based. Instead, these authors contribute to an image of more "boundaryless" careers; that is, careers that transcend the boundary of any single employer (Arthur & Rousseau, 1996).

One strand of recent career theory emphasizes the inherent danger of old assumptions about organizational benevolence. Dalton (1989) notes our tendency to see organizations as "simple and benign" when in reality they are "complex and dangerous" (p. 106), especially if we hold out false expectations that organizations cannot deliver. Those false expectations include the following: that hard workers will be taken care of; that people who make promises will be around to fulfill them; that specialized knowledge or past achievement means future security; and even that "career pathing" by "career development specialists" is plausible. A larger, more systemic problem concerns the need to reclaim the "civil society"—involving, for example, social life, health care, and pension arrangements—from our emergent dependence on the organization as benefactor (Perrow, 1996).

A second identifiable strand of recent career theory considers careers from the standpoints of reputation and employability, and thereby the mobility of personnel in a constantly changing mix of firms. Instead of lamenting the lost career opportunities in single organizations, people can rejoice in the new possibilities for interorganizational moves. A focus on building reputation over one's career can nurture employability regardless of the changing fortunes of any single employer (Kanter, 1989). Events (witness the changes within model large organizations such as Digital and IBM) have taught us that claims for employee career commitment based on continuing job stability and regular advancement are pretentious. In today's "intelligent enterprise," and in the emerging knowledge of society at large, people need not and should not fall for such claims. The intelligent career actor should know better (Arthur, Claman, & DeFillippi, 1995).

A third strand considers the psychological adjustment of the person. For example, Weick and Berlinger (1989) point out that although career scholars of the 1970s were bent on improving things within incumbent organizations, others were suggesting changes in the organization's make-up. In particular, the concept of the self-designing organization grounded in assumptions of continuous change and impermanence underpins a range of recent ideas about organizational adaptation and innovation. Yet the self-designing model challenges, even reverses, some traditional assumptions about organizational careers. Thus participants in self-designing organizations are advised, among other things, to decouple identity from the jobs they perform and to preserve discretion as a precondition for continuous learning. Mirvis and Hall (1996) extend the argument to suggest that an integrated career identity—spanning work and family issues and peaks and valleys in formal career achievements—is becoming essential. Psychological adjustment will be aided by peoples' greater influence over their employment contracts, and in turn over the unfolding of their lives.

A fourth recent strand addresses new family dynamics. On the one hand, demographic circumstances of both men and women experiencing work and family conflict call for more flexible employment arrangements (Bailyn, 1993). On the other hand, the need for greater organizational adaptiveness brings about new career possibilities for "Workforce 2000" (Arthur, 1992). Together, these arguments suggest that organizational and career futures need to be looked at simultaneously, rather than viewing career futures against organizational histories, or vice versa. The arguments also suggest a greater role for personal enterprise; for example, in working parents starting their own businesses or insisting on telecommuting arrangements. Increasingly, such enterprise appears necessary as an antidote to bureaucracy and as a spur to necessary innovation (Fletcher & Bailyn, 1996).

A fifth strand concerns networking. Personal networks have always seemed important for job search and for career revitalization in the face of job loss (e.g., Hirsch, 1987). However, recent ideas go further, in seeing networks as channels for new learning or as frameworks for amassing "social capital" and entrepreneurial opportunity (Raider & Burt, 1996). At a broader level, careers and the networks they weave can be viewed as integral to industry regions and the fabric that binds, for example, California's Silicon Valley together (Saxenian, 1996). By contrast, where large firms and their career systems have taken over, then deserted, an industry region—such as the engineering community in Springfield, Massachusetts—the challenge to reinvigorate such a region can be daunting (Best & Forrant, 1996).

Each of these alternative lenses casts new light on certain core assumptions of the past. Together, they suggest a quite different agenda for career research in the future. But before exploring an exclusively Western agenda, let us look again at data emanating from or about the East. What other career messages are in those data, and what new lessons might we draw from those images?

New Lenses on the East

What do our new career lenses suggest about Asian careers? Can they help us better appreciate the so-called Four Tigers of Hong Kong, Korea, Singapore, and Taiwan? Can they help us understand the resilience of Japan as an emergent high-wage, high-yen economy? Can they help us understand "new tigers"—such as Malaysia and Thailand—as they join the proclaimed "economic miracle"? Let us try to tease out some themes from recent reports.

Confucian Capitalism. We can begin on a note of Western humility. Prominent twentieth-century social scientists looked at Confucian culture and saw it as hostile to capitalist principles. Notably, those social scientists include Weber (see Berger, 1986) and Levy (see Wong, 1988). It seems, with hindsight, that we were looking at Confucian culture through unsympathetic Western lenses (Hofstede, 1991). Yet Confucian culture has hosted a highly instructive second case of industrial capitalism, one that confronts entrenched assumptions about the role of state intervention and the emergence of income inequalities (Berger, 1986). Moreover, the underlying values of Confucianism, including a commitment to education, belief in meritocratic personal advancement, capacity for hard work, and acceptance of deferred gratification (Henderson & Applebaum, 1992), all resonate with Western models of the career. The links among Confucian culture, capitalism, and careers call for our greater attention.

Competitiveness. Another reason to look again at the East, which we can draw from the recent work of Porter and his associates (Porter, 1990), is to explore the relationship between careers and national competitiveness. For Porter, two critical circumstances underlie national competitiveness: the presence of geographically concentrated industry regions and the intensity of competition within those regions. However, these two circumstances can readily be seen in career terms, the first as providing a natural and accessible labor market, the second as a spur to individual career achievement. Porter emphasizes how the two critical circumstances have fueled "rapid and continual upgrading of human resources"—read successful career development—in Japan. Also, workers and managers are committed to a "mutual investment in upgrading skills" (p. 411), and this upgrading of skills in turn provides "the driving force of diversification" (p. 407). Meanwhile, Korea compensates for "thin endowment of natural resources" with an "unusually disciplined and hardworking" workforce drawing on a high commitment to education and, of course, the "important underpinnings" of Confucian culture (p. 465). Asian experience suggests a direct link between careers and competitiveness that should be better understood.

Firm Size. The information on the critical issue of small firms has been available for long enough; for example in Clark's (1979) insightful book that preceded *The Art of Japanese Management* and *Theory Z*. The great majority of Japanese employment is in firms of 300 or less. It is difficult to get solid data at the large firm cut-off of 500 employees used earlier, but it seems that around 85 percent of all Japanese workers are in firms of under this size. Hong Kong, Taiwan, and Singapore all feature economies highly dependent on the flexible small firm (Cestells, 1992). South Korea has a higher proportion of large-firm workers, but political and worker unrest as well. India's industrial state experience of weak economic performance from large, state-run corporations lends further support for the significance of small independent firms (Kaye, 1988). Asia shows strong evidence that small firms, and career enactment through those firms are key contributors to economic success.

Job-Centered Learning. Learning is a career concept, at least in as much as learning occurs in the forty-plus years of working life beyond formal education. Again, the West appears to have initially floundered in trying to understand Japan, asking questions about formal training to which the answers were unremarkable (Ishikawa, 1987). But a closer look reveals, it is through the job and on the job that learning occurs, in big and small firms alike (Dore & Sako, 1989). The starting point for all the successful East Asian countries was unskilled labor. The pioneering investments were in "learning by doing" (Papanek, 1988); that is, in direct, unequivocal belief in people's career potential. The investments were not, as some Western observers would have it, in "picking winners" but rather in "picking teachers" (Hampden-Turner, 1990), or "learning how to win" (Cestells, 1992). The pursuit of new learning—spurred on by what Western careers scholars would recognize as mentors and relationship constellations (Kram, 1985)—appears continuous. However, many Western approaches to learning emphasize formal education, neglecting on-the-job experiences. The East has much to offer on the subject of learning as an everyday career experience.

Familism. There is another component to the Confucian inheritance already mentioned, namely, a high commitment to family and beyond to a notion of familism extended "to group, clan and nation" (Pye, 1988). And it is the extended, subtler aspects of familism that demand attention. One aspect is the heavy investment in women's education and employment in the Four Tigers and in East Asia generally (Wong, 1988). Another is the preference shown for dealing with nonfamily traders to avoid the liability of family obligation (Wong, 1988). "East Asian Familism" has also been depicted as underlying the subtle interplay between harmony and conflict (Freedman, 1971), or between cooperation and competition as we would tend to label them in the West. Perhaps the most arresting aspect of familism is the extent to which it underlies expatriate Chinese business success and career success across East Asia as a whole (Granrose & Chua, 1996). The suggestion that families drive careers, which drive business development, is a reversal of Western cause–effect assumptions about work–family relationships, and one that calls for closer attention.

Knowledge Flows. The unfolding of careers over time provides learning opportunities, and, as learning occurs, careers become vehicles for knowledge accumulation. In turn, knowledge accumulation underlies some remarkable Asian success stories. A recognized strength of Japanese career systems is that of process innovation, namely, taking an established product and making it more cheaply or better. One Western reaction has been to deplore the alternative "Silicon Valley" model of knowledge flows that result from career moves across firms (e.g., Florida & Kenney, 1990). Yet there are hints of other interfirm possibilities that have allowed Taiwanese firms to coordinate in flexible production and Hong Kong firms to network about key world market information (Cestells, 1992). The "spirit of Chinese capitalism" draws heavily on participants' external networks as media for information gathering and exchange (Redding, 1990). Meanwhile, large-firm layoff policies have encouraged a net outflow of knowledge from the Japanese large-firm sector into the small-firm sector (Koike, 1990). There is much still to be discovered about how careers affect knowledge transfer but much encouragement that further comparison between Eastern and Western careers will be fruitful.

Self-Interest. A concern with self-interest may come as a surprise, given the collectivist imagery of Japanese and other Asian behavior on which the West has been fed. However, recent views have argued that people's self-interest, as expressed through their career behavior, underlies the success of Japanese firms. One version emphasizes the explicit career incentives that are applied by Japanese firms and the firm-specific assets that people accumulate (Williamson, 1991). Another version argues that knowledge accumulation occurs as much in small firms as in large firms, and an estimate of only 10 to 20 percent of accumulated knowledge is firm-specific (Koike, 1990). So even if people remain loyal to single firms, there is an underlying labor market that lends meaning to loyalty and whereby firms acknowledge a person's value. In contrast, Western reliance on "deferred rewards" through pension vesting, vacation entitlement, and overall payment system arrangements seeks to resist rather than accommodate labor market effects (Arthur, Claman, & DeFillippi, 1995). We should learn more about the comparison between Eastern and Western firms' approaches to self-interest and their consequences.

THE WEST, THE EAST, AND CAREERS OF THE FUTURE

What, then, can be seen by looking through these established lenses and new lenses on careers and through their application to Asian careers in particular? The evidence is fragmentary and is offered to stimulate rather than to suppress further debate, so any conclusions drawn here must be tentative. Nevertheless, certain themes stand out and appear to call for some very different explorations in careers research than have been presumed in the past.

First, there is much to celebrate in the career concept. Its focus on and applicability to every individual serves as an antidote to other organizational scientists' aggregations about people at work. The insistence on the relevance of time, openness to interdisciplinary study, and parallel attention to subjective and objective views set the career concept apart from more limited social science concepts. Moreover, there is nothing in the career concept itself that implies a static, large firm, or a managerial emphasis. Indeed, the review in this chapter suggests the reverse—that careers research stands to flourish by dropping such restrictive assumptions, and in the process becoming more attentive to the working population at large.

Second, we can and must move on from stereotypical views of Asian careers that interfere with our greater understanding. Japan involves much more than a few large, stable companies offering lifetime employment.

The Four Tigers exhibit small-firm and family-firm characteristics largely ignored by Western inquiry. Confucian capitalism, with attendant themes of accumulating worker knowledge and intensifying network relationships, has succeeded in ways the West never used to imagine. The expansion of the Asian economic miracle to neighboring states reasserts the importance of underlying Asian career principles. There is much still to be learned.

Third, we can see connections between recent shifts in Western and Asian career themes. We are coming to accept that careers are inherently boundaryless as the career actors themselves and the stages (companies) for career performance change. However, it is in looking at what is going on around the stage that West and East may learn most from each other. Western career approaches idealize the star performers. Asian career approaches emphasize the learning available from any role in the production company. Western career approaches emphasize individualism. Asian approaches emphasize backstage support from invisible family and network contacts. Asian approaches also seem to better appreciate how new stages spring up in response to new combinations of career experience.

Fourth, we can emphasize the dynamic interdependence among careers by viewing careers as repositories of knowledge (Bird, 1996). Career studies have always held an affinity for the independence of the career actor; now the broader implications of independent action can be brought out. Given the significance of industry regions and of knowledge accumulation and transfer within them, it behooves us to learn more about how industry regions are sustained. It happens, somehow, through the learning and networking that constitute people's careers. Again, Asian career systems invite our greater curiosity.

CONCLUSION

Let us therefore look to the future, in the same manner we would expect from the individual consumer of careers research. The demise of the industrial state makes careers research emphatically *more* relevant than it was before. What other concept can unlock so much about the functioning and evolution of dynamic networks and industry regions within the new world order? What other concept has so much to offer in exploring the unfolding world of knowledge formation and exchange that underlies this new order? Let us pursue with urgency the kinds of answers comparison between Eastern and Western career systems can bring.

NOTE

Parts of this chapter originated in an address to the Careers Division workshop on Asian career concepts at the 1992 meeting of the Academy of Management, and certain ideas reappeared in the introductions to a special issue of the *Journal of Organizational Behavior* (Arthur, 1994) and to a subsequent book, *The Boundaryless Career* (Arthur & Rousseau, 1996).

In recent writing, I have avoided using organization to mean an entity in the sense of the organization and reserved the term to refer to a specific process or structure. However, that task seemed difficult to do here and would have set the language of this chapter apart from that of other chapters.

REFERENCES

Arthur, M. B. (1992). Career theory in a dynamic context. In D. H. Montross & C. J. Shinkman (Eds.), *Career development: Theory and practice* (pp. 65–84). Springfield, IL: Charles C. Thomas.

Arthur, M. B. (1994). The boundaryless career [Special issue]. *Journal of Organizational Behavior, 15*(4).

Arthur, M. B., Claman, P. H., & DeFillippi, R. J. (1995). Intelligent enterprise, intelligent careers. *Academy of Management Executive, 9*(4), 7–20.

Arthur, M. B., & Rousseau, D. M. (Eds.). (1996). *The boundaryless career: A new employment principle for a new organizational era*. New York: Oxford University Press.

Bailyn, L. (1978). Accommodation of work to family. In R. Rapoport & R. N. Rapoport (Eds.), *Working couples* (pp. 159–174). New York: Harper & Row.

Bailyn, L. (1993). *Breaking the mold: Women, men, and time in the new corporate World*. New York: Free Press.

Berger, P. L. (1986). *The capitalist revolution: Fifty propositions about prosperity Equality and liberty*. New York: Basic Books.

Best, M. H., & Forrant, R. (1996). Community-based careers and economic virtue: Arming, disarming, and re-arming the Springfield armory. In M. B. Arthur & D. M. Rousseau (Eds.), *The boundaryless career: A new employment principle for a new organizational era* (pp. 314–330). New York: Oxford University Press.

Bird, A. (1996). Careers as repositories of knowledge. In M. B. Arthur & D. M. Rousseau (Eds.), *The boundaryless career: A new employment principle for a new organizational era* (pp. 150–168). New York: Oxford University Press.

Burrell, G., & Morgan, G. (1979). *Sociological paradigms and organizational analysis*. London: Heinemann.

Cestells, M. (1992). Four Asian tigers with a dragon head: A comparative analysis of the state, economy, and society in the Asian Pacific Rim. In R. P. Applebaum & J. Henderson (Eds.), *States and development in the Asian Pacific Rim* (pp. 33–70). Newbury Park, CA: Sage.

Clark, R. (1979). *The Japanese company*. New Haven, CT: Yale University Press.

Daft, R. L., & Lewin, A. Y. (1993). Where are the theories for the "new" organizational forms? An editorial essay. *Organization Science, 4*(4), i–vi.

Dalton, G. W. (1989). Development views of careers in organizations. In M. B. Arthur, D. T. Hall, & B. S. Lawrence (Eds.), *Handbook of career theory* (pp. 89–109). New York: Cambridge University Press.

Dore, R. P., & Sako, M. (1989). *How the Japanese learn to work*. New York: Routledge.

Fletcher, J. K., & Bailyn, L. (1996). Challenging the last boundary: Reconnecting work and family. In M. B Arthur & D. M. Rousseau (Eds.), *The boundaryless career: A new employment principle for a new organizational era* (pp. 256–267). New York: Oxford University Press.

Florida, R., & Kenney, M. (1990). *The breakthrough illusion: Corporate America's failure to move from innovation to mass production.* New York: Basic Books.

Freedman, M. (1971). *Lineage and society: Fukien and Kwangtung.* London: University of London, Athlone Press.

Granrose, C. S., & Chua, B. L. (1996). Global boundaryless careers: Lessons from Chinese family businesses. In M. B. Arthur & D. Rousseau (Eds.), *The boundaryless career: A new employment principle for a new organizational era* (pp. 201–217). New York: Oxford University Press.

Hall, D. T. (1976). *Careers in organizations.* Pacific Palisades, CA: Goodyear.

Hampden-Turner, C. (1990). *Charting the corporate mind.* Oxford: Blackwell.

Henderson, J., & Applebaum, R. P. (1992). Situating the state in the East Asian development process. In R. P. Applebaum & T. Henderson (Eds.), *States and development in the Asian Pacific Rim.* Newbury Park, CA: Sage.

Hirsch, P. (1987). *Pack your own parachute.* Reading, MA: Addison-Wesley.

Hofstede, G. (1991). *Cultures and organizations.* New York: McGraw-Hill.

Hughes, E. C. (1958). *Men and their work.* Glencoe, IL: Free Press.

Ishikawa, T. (1987). *Vocational training.* Japanese Industrial Relations Series. No. 7. Tokyo: Japan Institute of Labor.

Kanter, R. M. (1989). *When giants learn to dance: Mastering the challenges of strategy, management, and careers in the 1990s.* New York: Basic Books.

Kaye, L. (1988, January 14). India's dinosaur legacy. *Far East Economics Review*, pp. 56–58.

Koike, K. (1990). Intellectual skill and the role of employees as constituent members of large firms in contemporary Japan. In M. Aoki, B. Gustavsson, & O. E. Williamson (Eds.), *The firm as a nexus of treaties* (pp. 185–208). Newbury Park, CA: Sage.

Kotter, J. P., Faux, V. A., & McArthur, C. C. (1978). *Self-assessment and career development.* Englewood Cliffs, NJ: Prentice-Hall.

Kram, K. E. (1985). *Mentoring at work.* Glenview, IL: Scott Foresman.

Mirvis, P. H., & Hall, D. T. (1996). Psychological success and the boundaryless career. In M. B. Arthur & D. M. Rousseau (Eds.), *The boundaryless career: A new employment principle for a new organizational era* (pp. 237–255). New York: Oxford University Press.

Naisbitt, J. (1995). *Megatrends Asia.* New York: Simon & Schuster.

New York Times (1996). The downsizing of America. (Seven-part series) March 3–9.

Newsweek (1996). Corporate killers. February 26, 44–48.

Ouchi, W. G. (1981). *Theory Z: How American business can meet the Japanese challenge.* Reading, MA: Addison-Wesley.

Papanek, G. (1988). The new Asian capitalism: An economic portrait. In P. L. Berger & H-H. M. Hsiao (Eds.), *In search of an East Asian development model.* New Brunswick, NJ: Transaction Publishers.

Pascale, R. T., & Athos, A. G. (1981). *The art of Japanese management.* New York: Simon & Schuster.

Perrow, C. (1996). The bounded career and the demise of civil society. In M. B. Arthur & D. M Rousseau (Eds.), *The boundaryless career: A new employment principle for a new organizational era* (pp. 297–313). New York: Oxford University Press.

Peters, T. J., & Waterman, R. H. (1982). *In search of excellence: Lessons from America's best-run companies.* New York: Harper & Row.

Porter, M. E. (1990). *The competitive advantage of nations.* New York: Free Press.

Prahalad, C. K., & Hamel, G. (1994). Strategy as a field of study: Why search for a new paradigm? *Strategic Management Journal, 15*(S), 5–16.

Pye, L. W. (1988). The new Asian capitalism: A political portrait. In P. L. Berger & H-H. M. Hsiao (Eds.), *In search of an East Asian development model* (pp. 81-98). New Brunswick, NJ: Transaction Publishers.

Raider, H. J., & Burt, R. S. (1996). Boundaryless careers and social capital. In M. B. Arthur & D. M. Rousseau (Eds.), *The boundaryless career: A new employment principle for a new organizational era* (pp. 187–200). New York: Oxford University Press.

Redding, S. G. (1990). *The spirit of Chinese capitalism.* Berlin/New York: de Gruyter.

Saxenian, A. (1996). Beyond boundaries: Open labor markets and learning in the Silicon Valley. In M. B. Arthur & D. M. Rousseau (Eds.), *The boundaryless career: A new employment principle for a new organizational era* (pp. 23–39). New York: Oxford University Press.

Schein, E. H. (1978). *Career dynamics: Matching individual and organizational needs.* Reading, MA: Addison-Wesley.

Sonnenfeld, J. (1984). *Managing career systems: Channelling the flow of executive careers.* Homewood, IL: Irwin.

Super, D. E. (1957). *The psychology of careers.* New York: Harper & Row.

Van Maanen, J. (Ed.). (1977). *Organizational careers: Some new perspectives.* New York: Wiley.

Weick, K. E., & Berlinger, L. R. (1989). Career improvisation in self-designing organizations. In M. B. Arthur, D. T. Hall, & B. S. Lawrence (Eds.), *Handbook of career theory* (pp. 313–328). New York: Cambridge University Press.

Williamson, O. E. (1991). Strategizing, economizing, and economic organization. *Strategic Management Journal, 12*(S), Winter, 75–94.

Wong, S. L. (1988). The applicability of Asian family values to other sociocultural settings. In P. L. Berger & H-H. M. Hsiao (Eds.), *In search of an East Asian development model* (pp. 134–152). New Brunswick, NJ: Transaction Publishers.

CHAPTER TWO

A Model of Organizational Careers in National Contexts

Cherlyn Skromme Granrose

Articles in The *Handbook of Career Theory* by Arthur, Hall, and Lawrence (1989) suggest that incorporating the concept of culture into career research may provide a particularly useful way of addressing the organizational and individual frames of reference commonly found in examinations of the concept of careers. This chapter responds to their suggestion to outline a model of careers applicable to different national cultural settings.

DEFINING A CAREER

American and European Perspectives

In American and European theory, a career is "the evolving sequence of a person's lifelong series of work related experiences and attitudes" (Hall & Associates, 1986). This is distinguished from a job, which is a single work position a person might hold at any one point in time. It is also distinguished from an occupation, which refers to a particular type of work a person might do in several jobs, such as being a dentist or mechanic. A career refers to the entire work life of a single person, including every job and every occupation held in that lifetime.

While a career is usually referred to as a multidimensional concept, two aspects of this concept appear repeatedly: the external career and the internal career (Derr & Laurent, 1989). The term *external career* refers to "the observable changing pattern of relationships between persons and organizations"; that is the realities, constraints, and pattern of jobs or organizational work positions a person holds during a lifetime. The term *internal career* refers to "the subjective aspects of a career, or the way a person thinks about his or her lifelong work experiences, including desires as well as evaluations." This bidimensional way of thinking about careers is the product of several distinct theoretical perspectives. The primary contributors include adult development, the sociology of work, vocational psychology, and human resources management (Sonnenfeld & Kotter, 1982; Ornstein & Isabella, 1993).

When looking across this breadth of career perspectives, certain characteristics emerge. First, a career is a characteristic of an individual which resides at an intersection between that individual and social organizations (Holland, 1973). The collective pattern of the careers of the members of an organization may also be examined for regularities, but if a career spans a person's work life, the individual career is not identical to these organizational patterns (Feldman, 1988; Hall and Associates, 1986). Second, much more is known about descriptive patterns of careers at the individual and organizational levels of analysis and much less about explanatory career processes that may involve cross-level or supra-organizational considerations (Schein, 1978; Osterman, 1988). Third, this work is embedded in American, rational, individualistic, goal-oriented, upward-mobility-valuing social science. This perspective may be inapplicable to the rest of the world (Wakabayashi, 1987).

Careers from an International and Cross-Cultural Perspective

Research on cross-cultural and comparative management reveals serious attempts to bridge the gap between Western-oriented views of career-relevant organizational behavior and views that may apply more broadly (Boyacigiller & Adler, 1991; Schein, 1984; Smircich, 1983). In order to move beyond ethnocentric conceptualizations of careers, Derr and Laurent (1989) have suggested examining the effect of different cultures on careers. The task then becomes one of integrating career theory with theories of culture to shape a perspective of careers appropriate for today's global environment.

A review of different theories of culture (Keesing, 1974) indicates that the term culture may be used to refer to "systems of socially transmitted behavior patterns or behavioral structures." Culture also refers to "cognitive systems of beliefs or meaning structures about aspects of social life"; for example, social categories, values, and rules or norms which may be differentially distributed across populations. These link the cognitive world of the individual with the collective ideas and behavior of social groups. Because theories of culture include both belief systems, such as those creating internal careers, as well as behavioral patterns, such as external careers, this integration seems possible.

Discussion of culture suggests that to expand conceptualization of careers outside of a single culture, we must find a way to (1) identify membership in a particular group; (2) incorporate variation in shared beliefs or knowledge systems; and (3) incorporate shared behavioral patterns into career theory (Boyacigiller & Adler, 1991). This integration forms the basis for outlining a model of careers that has as its foundation the interaction between individual work lives and collective beliefs and behaviors (i.e., national and organizational cultures).

PROPOSING A MODEL OF CAREERS IN NATIONAL CULTURAL CONTEXTS

Assumptions

Construct definitions and propositions must rest on certain assumptions about human nature, organizations, and science (Bachrach, 1989). First, this proposal recognizes the extent of variation and disagreement within a given organizational or national group as a characteristic of that group. Intragroup diversity and differential power of some group members in influencing the commonly held beliefs and behaviors are important aspects of groups that may be influential in careers. The implication of this assumption is that, in describing groups, the variety and complexity within a group must not be ignored in favor of describing average group characteristics.

Second, this model assumes that causal processes are multidimensional and include cognitions as well as actions. Work-related behavior observable by others and an individual's cognitions about work are considered equally important and necessary sources of information to define and explain the nature of careers.

Another assumption that this model uses is one of subjective utility. That is, it assumes that people generally act based on the perception that their actions will lead to valued consequences. The model does not assume that these perceptions are correct, only that people act on their perceptions when situations present action opportunities.

Levels of Analysis

Acceptance of careers as including both individual cognitions and observable job changes through time implies that the model must include at least individual and organizational levels of analysis. At the organizational level of analysis, an organization is defined most broadly as two or more people sharing common goals and having structured means to obtain the goals. Organizations include both profit and nonprofit institutions that have positions which individuals may hold for volunteer or paid work. The domain is drawn to include unpaid work because it is quite conceivable that a person might have a career consisting of unpaid positions in nonprofit organizations or in a family business with an identifiable pattern of position and task changes that would fit the theoretical definition of a career. In this case, the definition of these positions as "work" (rather than leisure or family roles, for instance) would rest with the individual.

This model has selected nation as the largest level of analysis, rather than industry, region, or ethnic culture. The selection of nation as a macro unit of analysis is not identical to using culture as a unit of analysis (Child & Tayeb, 1982). In this model, key characteristics of culture (i.e., shared patterns of beliefs and shared patterns of behavior) are defined in *each* level of analysis (thus, if a person's individual ethnic group membership is not identical to the majority of a nation's citizens, or an organization's location is not identical to its central headquarters, a mechanism exists for incorporating these cultural variations into the model).

This model describes careers in a national context to facilitate cross-national comparisons of careers and to facilitate descriptions and explanations of careers in multinational organizations. Since cross-cultural research of other phenomena guide this endeavor, it is crucial to clarify why and how a nation can be the important comparative cultural unit when other supra-organizational units with a shared culture might have been selected.

Although many cultural groups have identifiable shared belief and behavior patterns, nations have two characteristics that make them especially useful units for career research: (1) particular geographic locations with generally recognized physical boundaries; and (2) specific political–legal systems that formally regulate economic activity within this geo-physical space. The geographic unit is important because it provides the physical resources and limitations available for individuals and organizations to use in economic or work activities. The political–legal system is important because it defines the resources not available internally that may be imported, the products that may be exported, and the mechanisms that may or may not be used within the national boundaries to transform raw materials into marketable products or to provide needed services (Porter, 1990). Because these laws and regulations shape economic activity, they have a powerful impact on employing organizations and the careers possible within them. In addition, national units have a history of political leaders, economic development and recessions, wars, colonialism, and forms of economy that create a powerful shared history, even when political parties or national boundaries change as a result of these leaders and wars.

Within national borders, there are ethnic groups and regional industrial differences, and these differences are an important aspect of national
group diversity as mentioned earlier (Saxenian, 1994). However, these
regional differences must comply with some form of national regulation
as a unifying force. And it is the national laws that multinational organizations must recognize to do business in a particular subnational region;
it is the national government whose assistance is sought if regional differences or local laws block desired international trade.

Supranational industrial networks or conglomerates usually operate
across multiple national boundaries, and these levels of analysis might be
used for career comparison and explanation. Proponents of convergence
in comparative management argue that international managers moving
across borders are becoming homogeneous and may be members of an
"industrial culture" or a "global management culture" that differs from
any specific national or ethnic culture. This chapter adopts the perspective supported by Derr and Laurent (1989) that such discussions under-
estimate national differences in the group of managers with international
experience and overestimate the role and group size of these multinational
managers in the population of workers. Multinational career models do not
ignore the existence of such individuals and such career patterns.

Expansion of career concepts to include a national level of analysis significantly extends most intra-organizational careers described in past
theory and research and can address careers that include jobs in more
than one nation while still including the majority of managerial and nonmanagerial workers. Specific and unique aspects of supranational global
careers are left for the next expansion of career literature, when a larger
proportion of people have careers spanning so many different political or
national units that national laws and geographic boundaries no longer significantly affect shared work beliefs and behaviors.

CONSTRUCTS

Career concepts at each level of analysis (national, organizational, and
individual) are separated into four major constructs that have been useful
in defining and describing cultures. These constructs are *identity*, *beliefs*,
behavior patterns, and *processes*. For nations and organizations, the *shared*
characteristics are the ones selected for inclusion, whereas the personal
beliefs and behaviors remain in the individual level of analysis.

The constructs are defined so that each construct uses contributions
from psychological, sociological, and management theoretical perspectives on careers. Distinctions between constructs are based on theoretical
discussions of culture. Like most discussions of culture, the definitions are
broad and inclusive rather than narrowly specific. This option was chosen

because this is an initial outline of relevant factors, some of which might be eliminated with empirical evidence, others of which might be found relevant in some national settings but not others. The model proposes that *some* aspects of each construct will affect careers in every national setting. The construct definitions at each level of analysis are as follows:

National Level of Analysis

National Identity.   The unique characteristics of a nation which define it and its economic relationship to other nations. The career-relevant characteristics include political history, religions, number and relative size and power of ethnic groups, languages, political and trade relationships, and natural and technological resources that are available for economic activity.

National Career-Related Beliefs.   Evaluative and descriptive thoughts about work which are commonly held by members of a national unit, such as norms for appropriateness of gender, age, and ethnic group participation in the labor force, nationally shared beliefs about the meaning of work, and nationally shared work values.

National Career-Related Behavior Patterns.   National patterns of labor force distribution extending across time, organizations, and occupations. Examples of behavioral patterns include the structure and distribution of the labor force, as well as the structure and distribution of organizations in the nation.

National Career-Related Processes.   Formal and informal governmental policies addressing or structuring work behavior patterns. These include capitalist or socialist economy, policies oriented toward preservation of stability versus tolerance of social turbulence, provisions for educational preparation for work, as well as centralization or dispersion of economic planning and control.

Organizational Level of Analysis

Organizational Identity.   Characteristics which define the organization's position and resources, such as industry, history, size, and nationality of home office.

Organizational Career Beliefs.   Evaluative and descriptive beliefs commonly shared by organizational members which refer to positions and position holders, such as norms about position tenure, career paths, and position content.

Organizational Career Behavior Patterns.   Patterns of work behavior within positions and patterns of individual and group movement into and out of organizational positions.

Organizational Career Processes. Formal and informal organizational human resources policies and practice.

Individual Level of Analysis

Individual Identity. Characteristics of a person which define the self and his or her social position, such as gender, status, ethnicity, age, and education.

Individual Career Beliefs. Beliefs about work and its extension across the life span, including work values and aspirations.

Individual Career Behaviors. The rate, direction, and pattern of a person's position changes extending across the life span.

Individual Career Processes. Formal and informal mechanisms used by individuals to shape their work lives, such as career plans, goals, and strategies.

Cross-Level Constructs

Location. The nation in which an organization is operating and the nation and organizational position in which the individual is working at any one point in time.

Duration. The length of time an individual or an organization has occupied the same location.

Involvement. The extent to which an organization is related to (or sees its welfare as tied to the welfare of) a nation; or the extent to which an individual is related to a nation or to an organization.

Congruence. The extent to which beliefs, behavior, and processes are similar and not contradictory to each other.

Outcomes

National Outcomes. National economic and social well-being.

Organizational Outcomes. Organizational effectiveness and efficiency.

Individual Outcomes. Affect and motivation regarding the individual's ongoing work life.

In Table 2.1, the definitions of each construct are illustrated by representative measurable variables. The variables listed in Table 2.1 include those commonly appearing in Euro-American research on careers. It is quite possible that these may need to be revised as more cross-national research occurs outside of this tradition. The cross-level constructs are included to indicate processes or mechanisms whereby nations, organizations, and individuals influence each other because of physical proximity and integration, such as how long a person or organization has been in a particular place, or how important the nationality or organizational location is to the individual.

Table 2.1
Measurable Variables Related to Constructs

	NATIONAL	ORGANIZATIONAL	INDIVIDUAL
CAREER IDENTITY	Number of ethnic groups	Home office nationality	Gender
	Political and economic relationships	level of globalization	Ethnicity
	Economic Development	Profit/nonprofit	Nationality
	Resources	Industry	Education, SES
		Network memberships	Abilities
CAREER BELIEFS	Labor force participation norms	Norms about organization movement	Meaning of work
	Meaning and centrality of work	Value of positions	Work values Expectations of alternatives
	Work values		
CAREER PROCESSES	ED. and LFP Laws	HR Plans and policies	Career plans
	Capitalism/socialism	Reward systems	Career locus of control
	Centralization of economic policy	Career management systems	
	Unionization		
CAREER BEHAVIORS	LFP Rates	Position content	Rate, direction, and pattern of position changes
		Patterns of movement	
CAREER OUTCOMES	Effectiveness/ Efficiency	Effectiveness/Efficiency	Career and Job Satisfaction
	Satisfaction	Satisfaction	Work Motivation
	Growth	Growth	

PROPOSITIONS

The propositions suggested for this model describe necessary but not sufficient conditions of causality. Sufficient cause is often not identifiable, primarily because of the assumptions that these relationships are multidimensional and in many cases reciprocal.

Proposition of Relationships within Levels of Analysis

The relationship between identity, beliefs, behaviors, processes, and outcomes using the concepts of culture has been considered by psychologists examining individuals; microlevel sociologists and meso-level organizational behaviorists examining organizations; and anthropologists, macro sociologists, and organizational behaviorists concerning themselves with the national level of analysis. In Figure 2.1, these relationships within each level of analysis are illustrated.

The following discussion summarizes theoretical and empirical work supporting the propositions in this model. For a more detailed explanation at each level of analysis, the reader is directed to the original sources cited.

At the individual level of analysis, the theory of planned action (Ajzen, 1985) describes the relationships illustrated in Figure 2.1. In this perspective, the entire background or "identity," of an individual contributes to the formation of evaluative, normative, and probability "beliefs" that influence "processes," such as individual plans and intentions to act, which in turn influence "behavior."

In the career domain, London's theory of career motivation (1983) and Noe, Noe, and Bachhuber's empirical study of career motivation (1990) are

Figure 2.1
Relationships among Constructs within Levels

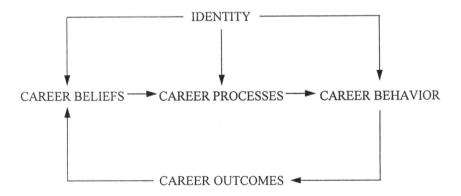

examples of descriptions of the relationships between identity, beliefs, behaviors, and outcomes. For example, London suggests that individual identity (needs, interests, and personality characteristics) is related to beliefs (desire for upward mobility, realistic or unrealistic perceptions about the self and the organization), which are related to processes (decision making, gathering information, and planning for the future) and behaviors (enacting career plans and coping with career obstacles), which have an impact on outcomes (motivation to work harder and feelings of career satisfaction). He also argues for the effect of outcomes on future beliefs and actions in his discussion of "retrospective rationality."

At the organizational level of analysis, theorists examining organizational culture discuss the impact of shared beliefs and values on organizational structure (processes and behavior) and outcomes. In a discussion of the roots of various aspects of culture in organizational science, Allaire and Firsirotu (1983) propose a mutual interaction system between beliefs, processes, and behaviors within the organization, as well as between the organization and the larger society and the individual, which fits the relationships proposed in this model.

Likewise, William Powell (1990, p. 300), in comparing market, hierarchical, and network forms of organization, argues that all organizational forms contain "key features" of norms, climate preferences (beliefs), transactions or exchange "behaviors," and communications and conflict resolution mechanisms (processes), which interact to produce a product or service (outcomes). In the literature examining nations, Gereffi (1989), Stewman and Konda (1983), and Hachen (1992) describe relationships between national characteristics and organizational identity factors, processes, and behavior such as those described in this model. Maruyama (1984) also outlines how nationally shared social beliefs about how the individual is connected to the group and how objective truth is seen are related to national and organizational management processes, behaviors, and outcomes.

Hofstede and Bond (1988) discuss in detail how Asian national cultural values such as belief in the teachings of Confucius lead to certain national and organizational processes and centralized hierarchical power relationships with specific leadership behaviors and positive economic growth outcomes. Similarly, Whitley (1990) compares the national social contexts of Japan, South Korea, Taiwan, and Hong Kong to describe the different organizational structure and policies used in Japanese *kieretsu*, South Korean *chaebols*, and Chinese family businesses. In each description, shared national values, laws, and resources shape nationwide industrial and organizational structures, and ultimately influence national economic success. Based on these representative discussions of similar patterns at each level of analysis, the following proposition is advanced:

P1. *Within the national, organizational, and individual levels of analysis, identity influences beliefs, processes, and behavior; beliefs influence processes; processes influence behavior; behavior influences outcomes; and outcomes influence later beliefs.*

Propositions of Relationships across Levels of Analysis

In their description of various perspectives on culture, Allaire and Firsirotu (1983) describe the interrelationships between the society, the organization, and the individual. In their conceptual framework, the ambient society's national culture influences organizational and individual beliefs and processes. Individual beliefs influence the organizational beliefs and processes that create individual and collective behavior as organizational and individual output.

Focusing particularly on the relationships between nations and organizations, Hofstede (1983), in his discussion of the cultural relativity of organizational practices and theories, offers a detailed argument of the influence of national cultures on several aspects of management in organizations. In non-Western discussions of the same principles, Chong (1987), Latham and Napier (1989), Whitley (1990), and Redding and Martyn-Johns (1979) examine several aspects of East Asia and identify particular societal cognitive systems, normative beliefs, and resident, immigrant, and colonial history, which are related to institutional and multinational management organizational processes that shape individual work values and career beliefs, career processes, and career behavior.

William Powell's description of organizations (1990) also supports the relationships between levels proposed in this model. He states that organizations are influenced by the national context because they act as "pieces of a large puzzle that is the economy" (p. 301). While each form of organization has its unique features, the individuals within an organization enact behaviors shaped by the organization. For example, within a hierarchy individual employees operate under work roles defined by higher level supervisors (p. 303). In turn, individuals shape the organization. For example, in network models transitions in organizational life occur through networks of individuals engaged in mutually supportive actions (p. 303).

In work regarding the relationship between national and organizational levels more specific to careers, Millman, Von Glinow, and Nathan (1991) indicate relevant environmental characteristics to consider in international human resources that indicate the impact of both the home country and the location country on organizational human resources processes which affect careers. In the same vein, Rosenzweig and Singh (1991) indicate that the across-nation environment, the within-nation environment, and the two-way conduit of influence between the parent company and the subsidiary influence organizational markets strategies, human resources strategies, and thus career management practices. Based on multiple discussions that shared national processes and characteristics shape organizations, and that locations of subsidiaries are shaped by the cultures where they operate, the following propositions emerge:

P2a. *National career beliefs, processes, and behaviors of the nation of organizational identity directly influence organizational career beliefs, processes, and behaviors.*

P2b. *If the nation of identity is not the nation of location, these relationships will be moderated by the effect of the beliefs, processes, and behaviors of the nation of location.*

Early discussions of the person/situation debate (see Mischel, 1977) provide a framework for considering the impact of nations and organizations on individuals. In his discussion of culture as an environmental context for individual careers, Schein (1984) states, "Even the idea of what a career is depends upon the culture in which it is embedded" (p. 71). Empirical support for these national differences in Europe is found in Laurent (1986).

The mechanisms of influence between the nation or organization and the individual career were addressed by Triandis (1973). Triandis proposed that cultural factors such as location, religion, language, and occupation influence national and organizational systems of roles and norms, which in turn influence cognitive structures, such as values. These influence intentions and behaviors, which lead to feedback on individual cognitions or beliefs.

In the domain of careers, Hall (1987) reviews how specific individual identity, beliefs, and processes (adult development, career decision making, and motivation); person–environment interaction processes (work–family interactions, mentoring); organizational processes (succession planning and career ladders); and national processes (hierarchies, occupational communities, and labor markets) influence individual and organizational career beliefs and outcomes. Empirical support for national variation in careers may be found in Gerpott, Domsch, and Keller (1988) and in work on expatriates (Tung, 1988; Black, Mendenhall, & Oddou, 1991). In this body of work, the national cultural context in which an individual career is enacted has definite effects on career aspirations, plans, and outcomes. Organizational norms and expatriate human resources policy processes can significantly mediate the effect of movement from one to another national location.

There is also evidence that individuals can influence the organizations to which they belong. For example, Kets De Vries and Miller (1986) discuss how various personality dimensions of executives influence the selection of strategies and functioning of their firms. Likewise, in Triandis's model (1973) individual cognitions influence roles and tasks in the organizational work setting as well. Given the evidence previously discussed, the following propositions are advanced:

P3a. *An individual's career beliefs, processes, and behaviors are influenced by the career beliefs, processes, and behaviors of the individual's nation of identity.*

P3b. *This relationship is moderated by the effects of the career beliefs, processes, and behaviors of the nation of individual location.*

P4a. *Individual career beliefs, processes, and behaviors are influenced by the shared career beliefs, processes, and behaviors of organizations in which individuals hold positions.*

P4b. *This relationship is moderated by the individual's location within the organization.*

P5a. *Individual beliefs, processes, and behaviors influence organizational beliefs, processes, and behaviors.*

P5b. *This relationship is moderated by an individual's location within the organization.*

The notion of congruence or fit influencing outcomes is central to a large body of literature arising from a systems theory perspective. Recent discussions of how this might operate in international human resources within and between the national and organizational levels appear in the Millman, Von Glinow, and Nathan (1991) work on organizational life cycles. The length of time an organization has operated in a particular setting or location and similarity between organizational culture, the home national culture, and the culture of the national location of a subsidiary each influence organizational processes and outcomes. Similarly, discussions of individual–organizational congruence (Granrose & Portwood, 1987; O'Reilly, Chatman, & Caldwell, 1991) indicate how individual values and expectations interact with organizational norms and incentive systems to produce individual affect and behavior. In these cases, the greater the match or congruence between individual career goals and plans and the organization's plans for the person, the more positive the outcomes of motivation and satisfaction.

London's theory of career motivation (1983) also emphasizes the role of integration or fit in understanding careers. He proposes that duration of exposure to a particular career environment is important to career outcomes. Considering these suggestions the following propositions are advanced:

P6. *The strength of the effect of national career beliefs, processes, and behaviors on organizational career beliefs, processes, and behaviors is a function of duration, involvement, and congruence between the nation and the organization.*

P7. *The strength of the effect of national career beliefs, processes, and behaviors on individual career beliefs, processes, and behaviors is a function of the duration, involvement, and congruence between the individual and the nation.*

P8. The strength of the effect of organizational career beliefs, processes, and behaviors on individual career beliefs, processes, and behaviors is a function of the duration, involvement, and congruence between the individual and the organization.

P9. The strength of the effect of individual career beliefs, processes, and behaviors on organizational career beliefs, processes, and behaviors is a function of the duration, involvement, and congruence between the individual and the organization.

P10. Greater congruence between levels and within each level of analysis will result in more positive outcomes.

In Figure 2.2, the cross-level relationships described by these propositions are illustrated.

Figure 2.2
Relationships between Levels

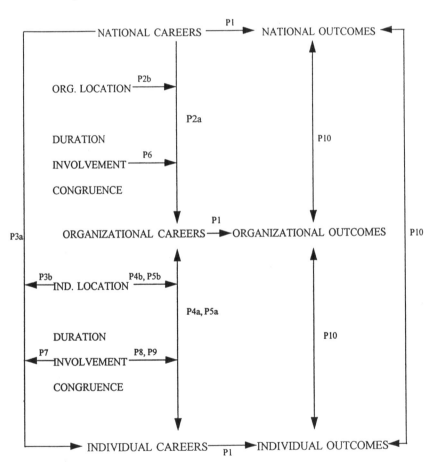

Because of the complexity of relationships when three levels of analysis are considered, it would be unusual for a single empirical study to address any but a few of these relationships. This network is illustrated to challenge future theorists to propose simpler, more elegant formulations, and to guide initial empirical work examining relationships between national, organizational, and individual careers previously ignored because they fell across multiple levels of analysis.

DISCUSSION

These assumptions, definitions, and propositions are an extension and combination of the existing Euro-American theoretical work on careers. They challenge the vocational and developmental psychological perspectives that a career is an individually determined and defined construct by proposing that organizational and national contexts shape individual career beliefs and behaviors. They also supplement the traditional organizational and sociological theoretical perspectives which assume that work must be paid, must occur within formal organizations, and must be determined solely by organizational structures, by including unpaid work, and by proposing that individual decisions and actions influence organizational policies and outcomes and that organizational structure and strategies can affect nationally shared beliefs and outcomes.

Examples given here are predominantly Euro-American because of the history of the field. There is evidence in research in cross-cultural theories of management to suggest that specific beliefs, processes, and behaviors will differ by nation. It seems clear that the first task is to identify *which* beliefs, processes, and behaviors in each nation are relevant to careers and how these interact. In part, the purpose of this discussion is to stimulate careful descriptive national analyses, from which generalizations across groups of nations may be drawn, and specific, unique national career characteristics may be identified. When this has been accomplished, much more specific corollaries of each proposition can be proposed.

Methodological Issues

Three types of methodological issues need to be addressed when translating this theoretical perspective into empirical work in non-Euro-American contexts. The first is a problem of definitions, the second is a problem of relationships between levels, and the third is a problem of statistical techniques.

Definition of Constructs.   Methodological problems of construct definition center upon clearly identifying what is and is not within the construct definition and determining that the constructs are discrete and nonoverlapping. Problems which arise in this area have been illustrated in the previous

discussion of the difference between culture and nation. Further problems of this type may occur in definitions of career-related beliefs and
behaviors. This is a particular problem in cross-national and cross-cultural research because the shared meaning and habits of measurement
response a given group may have are often different from the shared
meaning and shared habits of another group (Davidson, Jaccard, Triandis,
Morales, & Diaz-Guerrero, 1976). A growing body of literature on cross-
cultural research methodology can be of some help in pointing to the direction for solutions (e.g., see Berry, 1979; England & Harpaz, 1983; Hui
& Triandis, 1985; Steers, 1989).

The most serious methodological problem to consider when applying
this theory to Asian careers is the problem common in much cross-cultural research: Terms do not have the same meaning in different cultures.
If the basic definition of a career involves "the work domain viewed across
time," some distinctions not common in the United States need to be
made and others disappear. In Asian thinking, the dichotomous division
into external and internal careers may have a fuzzy or nonexistent boundary between the position held and the feelings and expectations about that
position. In addition, the divisions between career, job, and occupation
may be meaningless to some Asian people. Because both Chinese and
Japanese often use the same character to indicate job, occupation, and
career, linguistically, the distinction between these terms is not made in
everyday speech.

Distinctions between Levels of Analysis.   Although there are sometimes
comments in U.S. literature about fuzzy boundaries between national,
organizational, and individual levels of analysis, common cultural assumptions usually enable these distinctions to be used. Several problems arise
when these distinctions are applied to Asian careers. The first and most
general problem is related to the preponderance of collectivism in Asia
and individualism in North America (Triandis, Bontempo, & Villareal,
1988). Definitions of the unit of collectivism clearly differ across Asian
cultures, sometimes meaning family, organization, village, or nation
(Hofstede, 1980; Kim, Triandis, Kagitcabasi, Choi, & Yoon, 1994). Even
when we take into account national differences in collective societies, the
boundary between the individual and the group is seen as blurred or not
as important as group membership and loyalty. This minimizes the usefulness of the individual level of analysis, and in some cases suggests that
another group level of analysis (such as family) not included in the current theory could be used (Granrose & Chua, 1996).

The methodological problem of identifying relationships in a multi-
level, reciprocal network such as the one proposed here is in being forced
to give up unidimensional causal relationship models. This problem is
succinctly outlined by Blalock (1982). He calls for the development of

multidimensional models and research designs that incorporate, rather than ignore, the complexity of the reciprocal causal networks related to human behavior.

Statistical Problems.   The third problem, also addressed by Blalock, consists of finding methods whose assumptions match the model's theoretical assumptions. The current expansion of simultaneous equation models, catastrophe process models, and other nonlinear, multidimensional statistical techniques is making great strides toward matching models and analyses.

The multinational team whose work is reported in this volume began by using this general model as a framework to suggest the domain, constructs, and hypothesized relationships. The next step, collecting qualitative and quantitative data based on this framework, has been completed for one group of Asian nations, and some descriptive results are reported in this volume.

When these descriptive analyses are completed, we can use the initial responses to (1) determine a meaningful definition of a career in a particular context, clarifying how it is similar to or different from the general one initially proposed; (2) select the most important variables within each construct with meaning and relevance for each national context; and, finally, (3) propose new constructs, levels of analysis, and relationships which are country-specific modifications of the general framework. This is the process the Asian Careers Research Group is working on at the present time.

In summary, a theory has been proposed to link national, organizational, and individual perspectives of careers. Constructs have been defined based on examples used in the career literature as well as in the literature on culture. Propositions have been outlined that suggest that similar links occur within and across levels of analysis between identity, beliefs, processes, behavior, and outcomes. Domain limits and methodological problems relevant for empirical tests have been indicated. Empirical studies that address the ideas proposed here can be used in the future to develop a more appropriate, more specific, and more elegant model.

REFERENCES

Ajzen, I. (1985). From intentions to actions: A theory of planned behavior. In J. Kuhl & J. Beckman (Eds.), *Action-Control: From cognition to behavior* (pp. 11–39). Heidelberg: Springer.

Allaire, Y., & Firsirotu, M. E. (1983). Theories of organizational culture. *Organizational Studies, 5*(3), 193–226.

Arthur, M., Hall, D. T., & Lawrence, B. S. (1989). *Handbook of career theory.* New York: Cambridge University Press.

Bachrach, S. B. (1989). Organizational theories: Some criteria for evaluation. *Academy of Management Review, 14*(4), 496–515.

Berry, J. W. (1979). Research in multicultural societies: Implications of cross-cul-
    tural methods. *Journal of Cross-Cultural Psychology, 10*(2), 415–434.
Black, J. S., Mendenhall, M., & Oddou, G. (1991). Toward a comprehensive
    model of international adjustment: An integration of multiple theoretical
    perspectives. *Academy of Management Review, 16*(2), 291–317.
Blalock, H. M., Jr. (1982). *Conceptualization and measurement in the social sciences.*
    Beverly Hills, CA: Sage.
Boyacigiller, N. A., & Adler, N. (1991). The parochial dinosaur: Organizational
    science in a global context. *Academy of Management Review, 16*(2), 262–290.
Child, J., & Tayeb, M. (1982). Theoretical perspectives in cross-national organi-
    zational research. *International Studies of Management and Organization,
    12*(4), 23–70.
Chong, C. L. (1987). History and managerial culture in Singapore: Pragmatism,
    openness, and paternalism. *Asia-Pacific Journal of Management, 4*(3), 133–143.
Davidson, A. R., Jaccard, J. J., Triandis, H. C., Morales, M. L., & Diaz-Guerrero,
    R. (1976). Cross-cultural model-testing: Toward a solution of the etic-emic
    dilemma. *International Journal of Psychology, 11*(1), 1–13.
Derr, C. B., & Laurent, A. (1989). The internal and external career: A theoretical
    and cross-cultural perspective. In M. Arthur, D. T. Hall, & B. S. Lawrence,
    Handbook of career theory (pp. 454–471). New York: Cambridge University
    Press.
England, G. W., & Harpaz, I. (1983). Some methodological and analytical con-
    siderations in cross-national comparative research. *Journal of International
    Business Studies, 14*, 49–59.
Feldman, D. C. (1988). *Managing careers in organizations.* Glenview, IL: Scott,
    Foresman.
Gereffi, G. (1989). Rethinking development theory: Insights from East Asia and
    Latin America. *Psychological Forum, 4*(4), 505–533.
Gerpott, T. J., Domsch, M., & Keller, R. T. (1988). Career orientation in differ-
    ent countries and companies: An empirical investigation of West German,
    British, and U.S. industrial R & D professionals. *Journal of Management
    Studies, 25*(5), 439–462.
Granrose, C. S., & Chua, B. L. (1996). Global boundaryless careers: Models from
    Chinese family businesses. In M. B. Arthur & D. Rousseau (Eds.), *The
    boundaryless career: A new employment principle for a new organizational era*
    (pp. 201–217). London: Oxford.
Granrose, C. S., & Portwood, J. D. (1987). Matching individual career plans and
    organizational career management. *Academy of Management Journal, 30*(4)
    699–720.
Hachen, D. S., Jr. (1992). Industrial characteristics and job mobility rates. *Ameri-
    can Sociological Review, 57*, 39–55.
Hall, D. T. (1987). Careers and socialization. *Journal of Management, 13*(2), 301–321.
Hall, D. T., & Associates (1986). *Career development in organizations.* San Francisco:
    Jossey-Bass.
Hofstede, G. (1980). *Culture's consequences.* Beverly Hills, CA: Sage.
Hofstede, G. (1983). The cultural relativity of organizational practices and theories.
    Journal of International Business Studies, 14, 75–89.

Hofstede, G., & Bond, M. H. (1988). The Confucius connection: From cultural roots to economic growth. *Organizational Dynamics*, 5–21.

Holland, J. L. (1973). *Making vocational choices: A theory of careers*. Englewood Cliffs, NJ: Prentice-Hall.

Hui, C. H., & Triandis, H. C. (1985). Measurement in cross-cultural psychology: A review and comparison of strategies. *Journal of Cross-Cultural Psychology*, *16*(2), 131–152.

Keesing, R. M. (1974). Theories of culture. *Annual Review of Anthropology*, *3*, 73–97.

Kets De Vries, M. F. R., & Miller, D. (1986). Personality, culture and organization. *Academy of Management Review*, *11*(2), 266–279.

Kim, U., Triandis, H. C., Kagitcibasi, C., Choi, S., & Yoon, G. (1994). *Individualism and collectivism: Theory, methods, and applications*. Beverly Hills, CA: Sage.

Latham, G., & Napier, N. K. (1989). Chinese human resource management practices in Hong Kong and Singapore: An exploratory study. In A. Nedd, G. Ferris, & K. Rowland (Eds.), *Research in personnel and human resources management, Supplement 1, International human resource management* (pp. 173–200). Greenwich, CT: JAI Press.

Laurent, A. (1986). The cross-cultural puzzle of international human resources management. *Human Resources Management*, *25*(1), 91–102.

London, M. (1983). Toward a theory of career motivation. *Academy of Management Review*, *8*(4), 620–630.

Maruyama, M. A. (1984, January). Alternative concepts of management: Insights from Asia and Africa. *Asia Pacific Journal of Management*, pp. 100–111.

Millman, J., Von Glinow, M., & Nathan, M. (1991). Organizational life cycles and strategic international human resources management in multinational companies: Implications for congruence theory. *Academy of Management Review*, *16*(2), 318–339.

Mischel, W. (1977). The interaction of the person and the situation. In P. Magnuson & N. S. Endler (Eds.), *Personality at the crossroads: Current issues in international psychology* (333–352). Hillsdale, NJ: Erlbaum.

Noe, Noe, & Bachhuber (1990). An investigation of the correlates of career motivation. *Journal of Vocational Behavior*, *37*, 340–356.

O'Reilly, C. A., III, Chatman, J., & Caldwell, D. F. (1991). People and organizational culture: A profile comparison approach to assessing person-organization fit. *Academy of Management Journal*, *34*(3), 487–516.

Ornstein, S., & Isabella, L. A. (1993). Making sense of careers: A review 1989-1992. *Journal of Management*, *19*, 243–267.

Osterman, P. (1988). *Employment futures: Reorganization, dislocation, and public policy*. New York: Oxford University Press.

Porter, M. (1990). *The competitive advantage of nations*. New York: Free Press.

Powell, W. W. (1990). Neither market nor hierarchy: Network forms of organization. *Research in Organizational Behavior*, *12*, 295–336.

Redding, S. G., & Martyn-Johns, T. A. (1979). Paradigm differences and their relation to management with reference to South East Asia. In G. W. England, A. R. Negandhi, & B. Wilpert (Eds.), *Organizational functioning in a cross-cultural perspective* (pp. 103–124). Kent, OH: Comparative Administration Research Institute, Kent State University.

Rosenzweig, P. M., & Singh, J. (1991). Organizational environments and the multinational enterprise. *Academy of Management Review, 16* (2), 340–361.

Saxenian, A. L. (1994). *Regional advantages.* Cambridge, MA: Howard Press.

Schein, E. H. (1978). *Career dynamics: Matching individual and organizational needs.* Reading, MA: Addison-Wesley.

Schein, E. H. (1984). Culture as an environmental context for careers. *Journal of Occupational Behavior, 5,* 71–81.

Smircich, L. (1983). Concepts of culture and organizational analysis. *Administrative Science Quarterly, 28* , 339–358.

Sonnenfeld J., & Kotter, J. P. (1982). The maturation of career theory. *Human Relations, 35*(1), 19–46.

Steers, R. M. (1989). Organizational science in a global environment. In A. B. Chimezie & Y. Osigweh (Eds.), *Organizational science abroad* (pp. 293–304). New York: Plenum.

Stewman, S., & Konda, S. L. (1983). Careers and organizational labor markets: Demographic models of organizational behavior. *American Journal of Sociology, 89,* 637–685.

Triandis, H. (1973). Subjective cultures and economic development. *International Journal of Psychology, 8*(3), 163–180.

Triandis, H., Bontempo, R., Villareal, M. J., Asai, M., & Lucca, H. (1988). Individualism and collectivism: Cross-cultural perspectives on self-ingroup relationships. *Journal of Personality and Social Psychology, 54*(2), 323–338.

Tung, R. (1988). *The new expatriates: Managing human resources abroad.* Cambridge, MA: Ballinger.

Wakabayashi, M. (1987). *Career development under lifetime employment system in Japanese organizations.* Paper presented at Academy of Management, New Orleans, LA, August.

Whitley, R. D. (1990). Eastern Asian enterprise structures and the comparative analysis of forms of business organization. *Organization Studies, 11*(1), 47–74.

Chapter Three

Careers of Hong Kong Managers

Irene Hau-Siu Chow

This chapter looks at factors that influence managers' decisions about their careers in Hong Kong. These factors include external environmental factors such as the political and economic situation, the number of available jobs, and the unemployment rate. They also include organizational practices such as the types of human resources practices that provide different opportunities, incentives, and attractions. Individual factors such as age, sex, education level, family background, occupational aspirations, career expectations, commitment to work, and job satisfaction also play an important role in a person's career decisions.

This chapter also describes prevailing work-related beliefs and attitudes that influence the career decisions of a sample of Hong Kong Chinese managers. It looks at how Hong Kong companies view the careers of their employees. These attitudes and perspectives are reflected in the goals, policies, and practices for the career development of their executives. Using these perspectives, plus other published studies of Hong Kong managers, a concept of careers relevant to Hong Kong's own business society and culture will be developed.

Seventy-one Hong Kong Chinese middle managers were interviewed for this study. Some middle managers were from a local Chinese bank ($N = 20$) and two Hong Kong manufacturing companies ($N = 14$). The public sector was represented by staff from various departments of the Hong Kong civil services ($N = 19$). In addition, Hong Kong managers of three U.S. companies operating in Hong Kong ($N = 18$) were interviewed. These companies each had more than 200 employees and at least three managerial levels. Information about the organizations was gathered by interviewing human resources managers and by examining the line managers' perceptions of the organization.

MACRO-ENVIRONMENTAL SITUATION

In order to understand the career patterns of these managers, we must look at the external context of their careers. The constraints affecting Hong Kong human resources issues are a direct consequence of the events occurring outside the companies. By briefly clarifying the political and economic context in which these companies operate, it is possible to understand more of the rationale for human resources development affecting managerial careers in Hong Kong.

Hong Kong's Changing Economy

Hong Kong has an area of 400 square miles and a population of 6 million, with 2.8 million in the labor force (*Hong Kong Annual Report*, 1990). It has been a British colony that has adopted a laissez-faire economy in which the British Hong Kong government has kept intervention to a minimum. In the early 1950s, with the capital, machinery, and entrepreneurial skills of immigrants from China, Hong Kong established its manufacturing base in the textile and garment industries and further diversified into plastic and consumer electronics industries. Hong Kong's exports boomed in the 1960s, with an average annual growth rate of 15 percent. Hong Kong successfully transformed from a trade entrepôt after World War II into a leading exporter of light manufacturing goods in the 1950s and 1960s and a regional financial center in the 1970s. In the 1970s, Hong Kong further diversified into the financial services.

Exports grew at 13% a year from 1974 to 1983. The economic growth in Hong Kong, in real terms, was an average annual rate of 9.5 percent for the period 1961 to 1973, 8.9% for the period 1974 to 1983, and 7.8 percent for the period 1985 to 1990. In 1978, new economic forces as a result of China's new "open door" policy began to drive the Hong Kong economy. China's policies enabled Hong Kong to renew its entrepôt role and gave new impetus to Hong Kong manufacturers by encouraging joint ventures and out-processing activities in South China. China has overtaken the United States and Japan as the largest foreign direct investor in Hong Kong, investing about US$20 billion in 1992. However, after this substantial growth, the growth of GDP slowed down to 5.5 percent in 1994. In 1994, the GDP stood at US$116 billion and the GDP per capita was US$21,760. Between 1985 and 1990, the per capita GDP average growth rate was 6.8 percent. Consumer price inflation was high, and the average index fell from 12 percent in 1991 to 8.1 percent in 1994 (*Hong Kong Annual Report*, 1992, 1995).

Hong Kong has a workforce of 3.1 million, of which 62 percent are male and 38 percent female. In the early 1990s, the overall labor force participation rates were 79.1 percent and 46.8 percent for males and females, respectively (Census and Satistics Department, 1995). The highest female participation rate occurs in the 20–24 age group (83.4%). The manufacturing sector fell from 41.7 percent of total employment in 1984 to 17 percent in 1995 (*Hong Kong Annual Report*, 1996). During the past decade, manufacturers have taken advantage of China's open door policy to relocate labor intensive jobs to China, reaping the benefits of the lower land and labor costs there.

The influence of unions on wages and collective bargaining is weak. The declared union membership is only about 21 percent of the total workforce. The trade union movement is characterized as "fragmented," with many small unions. Industrial relations are very cooperative, and there is little overt industrial conflict. Hong Kong has a very low incidence of strikes, work stoppages, and working days lost. From 1990 to 1994, the average number of strike days was 8.8, and the average number of working days lost each year due to industrial conflict per 1,000 employees was only 1.87.

The Educational System

The educational system plays an important role in shaping later career opportunities. Nine years of compulsory education is provided to students between the ages of six and fifteen. Eighty percent of the relevant age group attend upper levels of secondary education. Ten years ago less than 5 percent of the 17–20 age group could receive tertiary education in Hong Kong. By 1994–1995, this figure had been increased to 18 percent, with 14,000 places available for the first year first degree courses in the tertiary institutions, funded by the Hong Kong government through the University Grant Committee. Since 1965, student numbers have increased more than tenfold, from 4,000 full-time students to about 47,540 in seven tertiary institutions. The expansion in tertiary education clearly demonstrated the government's commitment to a more stable supply of local talent. The number of students leaving Hong Kong for overseas studies was 13,348 (based on visa-issuing authorities) in 1995.

The Political System

In recent years, Hong Kong companies have been confronted with a number of significant political issues concerning the careers of their managers. These issues have important implications for organizational performance.

A political event that has had a significant impact is the return of Hong Kong to China by Britain in 1997. In response, a substantial number of managers have emigrated to the United States, Canada, or Australia, leading to a shortage of middle- and top-level managers. These managers claimed they were afraid of living under Communist rule whereby personal freedom may be curtailed.

When these data were collected, Hong Kong was a British colony. The Hong Kong Island was ceded to Great Britain under the Treaty of Nanking in 1842. In 1898, the New Territories were leased to Great Britain for ninety-nine years. The People's Republic of China (PRC) government insisted that these territories were seized illegally by the British through unequal treaties and that the entire territory must revert to China upon expiration of the ninety-nine-year lease in 1997. Under Chinese sovereignty, Hong Kong has become a Special Administrative Region (SAR) with a high degree of autonomy. In 1984, an agreement was signed between the government of the United Kingdom and the Government of the PRC on the future of Hong Kong (also known as the Sino-British Agreement or Joint Declaration).

The idea of "one country, two systems" was brought forward by Deng Xiaoping in 1984. Even though Hong Kong has come under the Communist Chinese sovereignty, the PRC government stated that it may retain its own capitalistic, economic, and political systems. The Provisions of Agreement guaranteed there would be no change in the existing systems for fifty years beyond 1997. In spite of this agreement, the return of Hong Kong to Chinese sovereignty has created a feeling of serious fear of political interference from PRC in the post-1997 period. The year 1997 took on the connotation of "doomsday" and created much uncertainty and anxiety among Hong Kong residents. Recent statistics indicate that annual emigration of the people of Hong Kong has increased rapidly. Government data suggest that about 62,000 people emigrated from Hong Kong in 1990. It is estimated that around 62,000 have left Hong Kong annually between 1990 and 1997. Most of the emigrants are young, well-educated, professional, managerial and executive staff. Companies were ill-prepared for this exodus of experienced middle managers and have filled these positions with junior and inexperienced managers who must be readied quickly to function in these positions.

The shortage of middle-level managers also means there are many opportunities for a highly mobile group of managerial employees. Companies are realizing that being proactive in providing career development opportunities for their executives is an effective way to retain their managers and to ensure a ready pool of individuals able to move into managerial positions. For example, a large Hong Kong hotel demonstrated this with an average rate of 1.4 percent staff turnover compared with the 58 percent industry average. It revealed that its practice was to promote the managers as well as rank-and-file employees from within the company (Wong, 1990). We will see how common these practices are in the following discussion of the organizational human resources process.

To summarize, Hong Kong's dynamic economic situation and the relations with China offer many opportunities for local managers. However, the return of Hong Kong to PRC sovereignty in 1997 created a feeling of uncertainty regarding the future of Hong Kong.

ORGANIZATIONAL CONTEXT

Human resources management practices affect individuals' career decisions, such as selecting their work organization and intending to stay in the same organization to pursue their careers. In 1992, there were 41,937 manufacturing establishments in Hong Kong, of which 87 percent employed fewer than twenty persons, and 95 percent had fewer than fifty employees (*Hong Kong Annual Report*, 1992). It is unlikely that companies of this size would be concerned with career development for their staffs.

In one large survey of more than 4,000 companies in Hong Kong, only 23.1 percent of the companies practiced human resources planning (Management Development Center, 1988). For those companies with human resources planning, about 60 percent of the 4,189 companies surveyed had problems with it. The problems included the following: planning failed to meet actual requirements (56.3%); planning could not be implemented in practice (40.1%); planning could not be done ahead of time (21.2%); there was insufficient knowledge of human resources planning techniques (14.7%).

Responding companies that did not practice human resources planning were asked to give reasons for not planning. The reasons these firms gave for not planning included the following: too small to be able to plan (68.9%); not familiar with human resources planning (25.6%); no resources (15.6%); do not believe in its usefulness (11.1%). When no human resources planning is done, internal and external labor policies are unclear. This situation is illustrated by data on how replacements are found. Sources of managers and supervisors included: outside hire (22%); internal promotion (25%); and fixed practices (40%). Given this general picture of the organizational setting in Hong Kong, we can now examine the specific policies of the organizations in the present study.

THE ORGANIZATIONS

Organizational Career Management Strategies

This study focused on large organizations in Hong Kong that generally provide more established processes for career planning and development for their employees than the average small Hong Kong firm. (In the small-to-medium-size Chinese organizations not included in this study, a career is largely left to the individuals themselves.) The human resources managers' efforts in larger Hong Kong firms included finding outstanding employees and grooming them for senior management. Three types of organizations were included: manufacturing, financial services, and government.

The two manufacturing organizations included in this study had home offices located in Hong Kong and also had production facilities in PRC. Manufacturing company A is organized into four departments with six levels of management. There is no official mission statement or management philosophy. Because the company was the first of its kind in the Hong Kong market, it has established good will and everyone in Hong Kong knows its logo. When a new plant was built in PRC production was relocated to PRC and staff was cut back in Hong Kong. The company employs 380 people. Most of them are male, with an average age of thirty-eight to forty years old. On the average, the managers have three years of experience. Local companies often rely heavily on on-the-job training, with managers mainly promoted from within; however, this company has hired three consultants and technicians from Taiwan.

There were no formal career paths for managers in firm A. The entry qualifications were secondary school graduation with some relevant working experience. Most started as junior level officers and took about ten years to move up to managerial positions. Proven performance, ability, and seniority were required to move up the organizational hierarchy. Employees perceived that the opportunities and prospects in the manufacturing sector were not very good compared to other sectors. Even so, people often left simply because they could get better paying jobs elsewhere. Manufacturing company B is a large machine tools company with operations in PRC and Taiwan. It has grown from a small family-owned company into a sizable company over the past three decades, with 1,400 employees and five levels of managerial ranks organized in six departments. The management philosophy here emphasized pursuit of excellence and work dedication. Unlike the other manufacturing company, this organization offered a very comprehensive training scheme, ranging from craft/technician trainee up to engineer trainee programs. Practical, hands-on experience was considered more important than educational qualifications for hiring and promotion. That is why most of the section heads and senior technicians came from the trainee scheme. A formal human resources planning system had been implemented. The objectives reported by the human resource managers were "to procure, retain and motivate employees and to provide adequate, qualified employees for business expansion."

The third organization was the Hong Kong civil service. The Hong Kong government, the largest employer in Hong Kong, employs more than 190,000 civil servants, about 7 percent of Hong Kong's work force, or 3.3 percent of the total population. The public sector accounted for 20 percent of the total GDP of the Hong Kong economy in 1990–1991. The administrative structure in the Hong Kong civil service is divided into three classes, namely, administrative, executive, and clerical classes. There are about 440 grades or job categories, with 1,200 ranks and job levels.

The percentage of employees leaving the civil service, including those resigning and retiring, was about 5.5 percent in 1990–1991. The turnover rate in civil service has stabilized at around 5 percent. The number for 1989–1990 was 10,790. This figure was relatively low compared with more than 10 percent in the private sector. However, it represented a threefold increase since 1985–1986. According to a survey conducted by Cooper and Lui (1990), 15.5 percent of the senior civil servants indicated that they would be leaving the service by the year 1997 through early retirement or expiration of contracts.

The present civil service career package may not be totally appropriate for the retention of professionals. Retention strategies used by the public sector include providing good benefits and working conditions, promoting teamwork, offering appreciation, offering broad job experience, providing career opportunities for the future, and offering career training.

The human resources managers interviewed for this study reported that 90 percent of the time the public sector promoted their staff from within to fill most positions. The private sector used a combination of external hire, promotion, and transfer to fill most positions.

Formal human resources planning was perceived as ineffective or not done by most line managers. Two-thirds of the respondents in the manufacturing companies reported that they were not aware of or they believed they had no formal human resources planning process in their organizations.

The fourth organization studied was a bank. Hong Kong has emerged as a general financial center. A manpower survey covering 496 banks and financial institutions was conducted by the Vocational Training Council, in December 1992 (Bank Training Board, 1992). The survey showed a workforce of 74,306 persons working in the banking industry, an increase of 4,027 over the previous year. The growth in the size of banking personnel denotes that the banking industry was still expanding. The distribution of the workforce was 13 percent in managerial ranks, 22 percent in supervisory jobs, and 65 percent in clerical and supporting staff. Employers reported 1,365 vacancies in the banking industry, representing 1.8 percent of the total workforce. The banking industry has been facing a high staff turnover rate. The total number of persons leaving was 15,237 (20.5%). The reasons given for leaving included taking up a nonbanking/nonfinance job (20%), taking up another banking/finance job (12.8%), and emigration (5.4%). Retirement accounted for only 1.3 percent. In view of the high staff turnover rate and the rapid development of various financial and banking services, investment in human resources is of great importance.

A local Chinese bank was chosen to represent the service sector in the present study. The bank was organized into corporate planning, marketing, international business, and administration, with twenty-nine branches and more than 800 employees. The levels of managerial hierarchy, from bottom to top, were executive officer, submanager, manager, senior manager, chief manager, and managing director. The distribution of the workforce in this bank was 10 senior managers, 80 middle managers, 200 officers, and the rest clerical and supporting staff. The managerial positions were dominated by males. The bank's home office is in Hong Kong.

The banking industry relies on internal promotions. The preferred level of qualifications are university degrees and professional qualifications for the managerial grades and upper secondary school level for the clerical grade staff. In this organization, it takes twenty years to move from clerk through executive trainee, supervisor, and officer to manager. Normally, managers will stay in the same position between five to seven years, depending on their capability. In 1990, 189 staff resigned, including one senior manager and nine middle managers. The majority of those who resigned were officer rank (6%) and clerical staff (58%). Among those who resigned, 55 percent had been with the bank for less than one year, and 20 percent of them had joined the bank for one to two years. The reasons given for resignation were changing field (32%) and pursuing further studies (32%), followed by getting a higher salary and/or better prospects elsewhere (13%).

The low confidence in the future of Hong Kong affected the retention of staff. Solutions to the confidence and turnover problems offered by the bank's human resources manager include promotion, higher salary, and affiliation with a foreign bank.

Organizational Career Paths

On the average, managers stayed in the same position about four to five years. In government, the first two to three years were a probation period for new recruits. Thereafter, vertical mobility progressed through the subgrades. Following a formal career path or pattern was more prevalent among respondents and their colleagues in the public sector. Respondents reported only informal career paths in the banking industry. There was no single common career pattern reported by human resources managers in the manufacturing firms.

The reasons managers leave their organizations, as perceived by the human resources managers in the manufacturing companies are the following: better opportunities are found elsewhere (50%); the nature of the job does not meet personal goals (20%); the job requires repetitive duties

(20%); no further promotion is envisioned (10%). The reasons given by Hong Kong employees of U.S. companies were dissatisfaction with job tasks, pay dissatisfaction, and unsatisfactory location.

Organizational Career Management Activities

Some form of career management activities existed in all organizations; however, many may not have been fully implemented. Both human resources managers and line managers were asked whether a range of career development activities usually undertaken for managers was (1) not available, (2) available informally, or (3) available formally. The public sector offered more career management activities than the private sector. The majority of these activities were available formally in the civil service. The manufacturing companies offered fewer career activities, and these activities were either informally available or not available at all. Chinese managers working for U.S. companies in Hong Kong reported that job posting, career testing, coaching/mentors, and career planning workshops were not available, whereas career information and leadership, or skill training workshops were formally available. Regarding the availability of career management activities, performance review was the only activity available across all three industries. Job posting and career information were formally available in the private sector. These activities in career planning and development increased employees' knowledge, aspirations, attention to career development, planning, and commitment.

A discrepancy existed between what was reported by the human resources managers and what was perceived by the line managers. Human resources managers reported that more career management activities were available in organizations than those perceived by line managers. Counseling, career testing, and job/organization information were said by the civil service branch to be available formally in the public sector. However, civil servants were not aware of such activities. The same situation occurred in the banking organization. Human resources managers reported that job posting and career information was available formally, but employees were not aware of such activities. These discrepancies emerged when we compared the responses reported by human resources and line managers. It is obvious that there is insufficient understanding of the kind of work human resources managers perform.

Human resources and line managers also were asked what informal mechanisms organizations used to influence employees to have careers the organization wanted them to have. Organizational influence was measured by nineteen items based on organizational practices (Gutteridge, 1988) and influence strategies (Kipnis et al., 1980). The organizational influence discrepancies between human resources managers and perceptions of line managers existed across all the industry sectors. The items with the largest discrepancy included "indirectly threaten," "promotes teamwork," "uses family connections," and "treats like family."

The manufacturing firms were perceived as less likely to use pay, fringe benefits, working conditions, employee influence on important decisions, and future opportunities and training to entice their workers to choose a particular career desired by the organization. In general, the manufacturing firms were believed to provide less favorable career development opportunities. Company A had to pay a hardship allowance to compensate for the adverse working environment. One of the problems quoted by one human resources manager was that "good quality managers come and go; they don't stay long. Once they get a better opportunity elsewhere, they'll leave."

Perhaps an indicator of the importance of training as a career development strategy is the amount of money organizations were willing to spend on it. In an earlier survey, 55 percent of companies spent only 1 percent of payroll or nothing on training (Kirkbride & Tang, 1989). An interim report from the Management Development Center concludes that Hong Kong companies "spend relatively little effort in management development . . . . Some of them did not believe in the importance or benefits of management development" (Management Development Center, 1988).

Promotion Criteria

The Chinese family business is the dominant form of business in Hong Kong. In these family businesses, top management has absolute authority and power. They tend to use less formal planning and fewer control systems. The reward system is not based on performance but on seniority and loyalty. Family or personal ties such as classmates or people graduating from the same school become important factors in promoting managers into high ranking positions.

The nepotism in business has gradually faded away as organizations have become more formalized, but, in general, a special relationship is still an important consideration in promoting managers to higher ranking positions. In spite of these traditional customs, when the human resources managers were asked about important criteria for promotion, 70 percent believed that on-the-job performance was the most important criterion for promotion. Seniority was also considered an important criterion, but they said politics was not important. According to the human resources manager, promotion preference for the bank would be given for capability, loyalty, and being good to subordinates. "Being creative, being willing to change, and improving old operations are also important," he claimed. For manufacturing organizations, human resources managers' criteria included quality and quantity of production, suitable related experience, and good human relations skills. Line managers perceived that the criteria were the quality and quantity of work, the amount of skill and job knowledge, attendance, discipline/safety, cooperation, cleanliness, initiative, ability to learn, possessing common sense, and leadership quality. For the public sector, good performance, merit, and effectiveness of task execution were considered critical by the civil servants.

One Hong Kong human resources manager of a U.S. firm said, "The time between promotions is shorter here than in the United States. To keep good employees I will create a new job to give them more to do. Every two to three years a manager will either receive a promotion or a change in job responsibilities."

An Asian-Pacific regional human resources manager of another U.S. firm explained the difference this way: "In Hong Kong we can talk more openly about career options and movements than we can in our Japanese operation, where people become upset if you move people outside of the seniority system."

To summarize, career development activities and human resources management practices varied across the types of organizations included in the present study. To a certain degree, a discrepancy existed between what was reported by human resources managers and the perceptions of line managers. Although there were typical career paths in government service and banking, most organizational career management actions were informal. The organizations were doing very little in formal activities to manage their employees' careers.

THE INDIVIDUALS

Individual Characteristics

The average age of the respondents was forty-one and a half years old, with a range of twenty-seven to sixty-one years. All of the respondents were Chinese. Seventy-seven percent of them were male, and 77 percent were married, with an average of two children. The respondents' education level was evenly distributed, with most having polytechnic or bachelor degrees. Most of these managers were bilingual, speaking both Chinese and English. The occupations of civil servants were spread over (1) the professional/technical area—technician, engineer; (2) general grades—executive officer, teacher; and (3) disciplinary forces—immigration officer, prison officer, and police officer. Those employed in U.S. firms were slightly younger, had fewer children, and were more likely to have obtained a college degree.

The External Career

The "pay level survey for the manufacturing sector" conducted by the Hong Kong Industrial Relations Association (1991) revealed that 26.6 percent of the staff in the manufacturing sector who resigned during 1990 had less than three month's service, and 52.5 percent of the resignees had less than one year of service. For lower level workers, the turnover problem was more serious. Clerks, technicians, storekeepers, and engineers had the highest turnover during the first six months of 1991.

In the present study, the average respondent worked 47 hours per week and had 14.7 years in the labor force. They had worked on the current job for an average of 4.2 years. The number of organizations worked for was 4.2, with a range of 1 to 7. One respondent recalled,

I joined a large MNC because I wanted to work and gain experience in a large organization. Two years later, I started to look for a better job and helped my friend with his business to get access to more business contacts. Later, I moved to banking and took up the position of Assistant EDP Manager. I am always willing to take up new challenges and to try to learn more.

The civil servants had longer organizational tenure and job tenure. The average annual salary of respondents was US$49,000. The average number of promotions the respondents had received was 3.1. The external career track records of the respondents are given in Table 3.1. These figures reflect the wide variation in career pattern in this sample.

Table 3.1
External Careers of Hong Kong Managers

Career	Hong Kong Firms				U.S. Firms
	Total	Civil Service	Service	Manufacturing	
	(n-71)	(n-19)	(n-20)	(n-14)	(n-18)
Years in labor force	14.7	15.6	16.2	12.1	13.4
Number of Organizations worked for	2.4	2.1	2.3	3.1	3.7
Longest org. tenure	10.0	11.2	11.2	7.1	7.5
Shortest org. tenure	2.2	2.3	2.6	1.8	1.9
Number of promotions	3.1	2.0	4.2	2.6	2.4
Longest job tenure	6.1	9.3	5.1	4.1	3.7
Shortest job tenure	1.6	1.7	1.8	1.3	1.2
Current job tenure	4.2	6.5	3.1	3.3	2.1
Org. tenure	11.1	14.1	13.1	4.9	6.0
Hours/week worked	46.9	45.3	48.7	46.3	49.3
Number of Levels to top	3.4	4.5	3.9	2.7	1.5
Expected org. tenure	8.1	8.8	10.1	4.0	6.6
Will accept lateral transfer	3.0	3.5	2.7	2.7	3.3
Will accept transfer with promotion	3.3	3.7	3.1	3.0	3.9

Note: All tenure items are expressed in years. Willingness to accept a transfer was rated on a 5-point scale where 5 equals very willing.

The external environment, such as the number of employment opportunities, may affect job mobility, the level of organizational commitment, and the shape of external careers. Despite unfavorable external factors, Chow's (1990) cross-sectional study of middle managers found that the level of organizational commitment in Hong Kong was much higher than that reported in the United States, Canada, Korea, and Japan. This was partly because of more motivating and challenging jobs. Wong's (1992) study, based on Hong Kong nonsupervisory employees, reported a much lower level of organizational commitment after controlling for the effect of motivating potential score (Hackman & Oldham, 1976). The turnover rate was generally higher among the nonsupervisory employees.

Corporate culture and human resources practices also affect the level of commitment, loyalty, and identification that individuals exhibit toward their organizations. Chinese managers employed in U.S. subsidiaries in Asia had significantly higher organizational commitment than those employed in Chinese organizations. U.S. subsidiaries were perceived to be better managed compared with Chinese organizations. Working for a foreign company may be perceived as a passport to security, as well.

Mobley, Griffith, Hand, and Meglino's (1979) model indicates that the perceived probability of obtaining desirable alternatives is related to organization turnover. Mobility can also be viewed from the opportunities available internally or externally. Internal opportunity measures the possibility of changing from one job to another equal or better job within the same organization. External opportunity measures the possibility of obtaining an equal or better job in some other organization. Respondents in the banking industry and foreign companies found it relatively easy to change jobs both internally and externally. The internal opportunity for respondents from the manufacturing industry was quite restricted but estimates of their external opportunity were optimistic. More than 70 percent of the civil servants reported it was almost impossible, or at least very difficult, to find jobs elsewhere. One respondent pointed out that "practices and procedures in government are different from those in the private sector." Another remarked that "the experience acquired in the public sector has little commercial value." Eleven out of the nineteen civil servants had not changed job level. Five of them changed job level only once. However, within the civil services, horizontal mobility (i.e., shift from one post to another at the same level) is more common. An example of the civil service career pattern is quoted as follows:

I started my first job as electric technician after graduated from university. I stayed there for nine months. I left due to low salary and found a more interesting job in an American firm. I stayed only for half a year because of low promotion prospects. After working for two organizations, I joined the government, starting as an engineering assistant. The reasons for joining the government included good prospects and chance of obtaining a scholarship for further studies. I stayed in the position for six years (including three year's study leave) before being promoted to assistant engineer. After four and half years, I was promoted to engineer. At the age of forty-six, I have been promoted to a senior engineer for two and half years and have earned a good salary. This career path is considered to be successful. There are four levels to the most senior person. However, further promotion may be difficult due to the limited number of chief engineer posts.

Managers in the private sector were not restricted to a single organization. As an example of a typical career path of someone in a U.S. firm, one Hong Kong manager told the following story:

I began as a file clerk for a British firm. When my supervisor left to join this company, he got me over here to this company. Then I got promoted to his position, then I was given more responsibility. The manager in country B got sick, so I was sent there. When this company merged, I was transferred to country C. Two years later I was transferred to country D, and last August I was transferred back to Hong Kong and promoted to this position.

Half of these managers had worked for their current employers for two years or less. On this end of the spectrum, here is a typical example:

My first job was as a cost analyst. I left that job to go back to school for a year. Then I worked for company B (in a different country) as a project engineer for two years and as a business analyst and then as a planning analyst for three years. I moved to Hong Kong and worked for a consulting company (C), doing business development in China for a few months. I worked for (company D) in financial management for two years. I joined this company (E) one and a half years ago as a business planning advisor.

Most managers have changed organizations during their management careers. The study reported here has shown that the movement of managers among organizations is important in the process of achieving career advancement in the private sector. Private sector employees are more willing to take the risks and capture every opportunity for advancement and to experience something new. Each time a person changed jobs, he or she would inflate his or her pay package by 20 to 30 percent.

The Internal Career Beliefs

Norms and Values of Hong Kong Society.   Based on Hofstede's (1980) Value Survey, Hong Kong is classified as high in power distance, low in uncertainty avoidance, low in individualism, and medium in masculinity of its values. Yeh (1989) did not agree with Hofstede's treatment of the Chinese (Hong Kong, Taiwan, and Singapore) values. He has argued that the Chinese are more individualistic than is indicated by Hofstede.

The general perception of managers is that Hong Kong is a place full of opportunities with a high degree of social openness. In another large social survey of 786 respondents on the most important ingredients for a happy life, the Hong Kong respondents' perceptions of happiness were very personal and individualistic. Good health (36.5%) was the most cherished value of the largest number of respondents. Money was the second most commonly named value (16.3%). The emphasis placed on certain Confucian values, such as peace of mind (12.7%) and filial piety (8.5%), may reflect the lingering influence of traditional Chinese culture. Then followed freedom, valued by 8.1 percent, and career, valued by 6.9 percent. Despite the importance of the family in Chinese society, love and marriage was given a relatively low priority. The overall degree of satisfaction with personal life was 3.5 (1 being very dissatisfied, 5 being very satisfied). Hong Kong people were most satisfied with their family life (3.7), followed by other personal social ties such as friends, relatives, leisure, work, and educational attainment (2.8). Because employees in the territory have a very heavy work load, Wong (1992) reports that they have become more conscious of their health, diet, and leisure.

In a general social survey of 413 relatively young respondents (50.8% of the respondents were less than thirty-five years old) on their attitude toward work in general, there was a consensus in recognizing the importance of work in their lives: 83.8 percent replied work was "important or most important." For the most important consideration when choosing a job, half of them picked salary (50.3%). Job content (12.9%) and promotion opportunity (12.4%) were the second and third most important, followed by working environment (8.4%). Hong Kong people emphasized income and valued salary highly in the process of job selection. In general, the Hong Kong Chinese are hard working and motivated. A significant number of the respondents (30.8%) are pursuing further studies after work to improve their of qualifications or to acquire new knowledge for promotion (Lui, 1992).

In another study, views from the public and private sector employees were sought (Chow, 1988). Advancement opportunity, higher earnings, and security were considered the most important career goals. This is consistent with the more materialistic, extrinsic, and instrumental orientation of the Hong Kong people. Such findings are also consistent with Shenkar and Ronen's (1987) study on work goals.

In this study, Hong Kong managers valued promotions most highly. Training ranked second, followed by cooperative co-workers and earnings. Among the least important work goals were recognition, geographic location, security, benefits, and favorable physical working conditions. The least important work goal was time for nonwork activities.

Results revealed that respondents in this study were quite happy with their jobs; half of them felt "satisfied or very satisfied." Only 12.9 percent gave a negative answer. They were least satisfied with promotion (28.6%) and pay (28.5%). When they were asked to evaluate their achievement in their work history as a whole, 70.6 percent gave positive answers (i.e., they felt that their career had "somewhat improved or improved a great deal"). When asked about the possible impact of the 1997 issue on their career, slightly more than half (56.1%) expressed the view that changes brought about by the 1997 issue would affect their career development. The overwhelming majority were pessimists, with 91.6 percent believing the changes would be detrimental.

The meaning of work and the importance of work were measured by the following questions: (1) How much does work contribute to the way you feel about yourself? (2) How much has work influenced the kind of person you are? On a scale from 1 to 5, the average scores were 4.1 and 3.7, respectively. The importance and significance of work in life was rated 3.9. Life satisfaction was rated 3.65.

Respondents were asked to draw a picture to represent their careers in their working life. There was a general upward trend for most respondents. The career path was considered to be successful as it progressed from junior to senior positions. Respondents from the manufacturing sector experienced more ups and downs in their career paths. For instance, one respondent changed jobs seven times to different organizations, both local and foreign companies. The reasons for quitting included leaving for better working conditions, personnel problems, lack of job satisfaction, and layoff due to a cutback in operations. His career path shows a twin peak. The first peak occurred when the respondent was promoted to the managerial rank from a technical job. He said he faced new challenges and learned a lot from that work experience. The second peak occurred a few years later due to the development opportunities provided by the company. He achieved all his predetermined targets and goals and experienced a record high level of satisfaction and success. Thereafter, the respondent faced a critical turning point of being laid off due to a cutback in production operations. He is disappointed with the corporate culture and management style in his present organization.

Career Goals. For many people, career decisions start with having some idea of a few general career goals. In the structured questions, managers were asked to rate the importance of each of twenty-three possible career goals on a 1 to 5 scale. Table 3.2 shows the importance of career goals among respondents in three different sectors.

Respondents valued income, promotion, and personal growth as well as prestige, achievement, skills, and meaningful work. Convenient working hours, residence location, and keeping busy were among the lowest ranked career goals for managers. In Hong Kong, only lower level operative workers would consider working hours, location, and keeping busy important in looking for jobs. Hong Kong managers working for U.S. firms considered intrinsic values such as use of skills and education, creativity, meaningful or interesting work, independence or autonomy, achievement of challenges, and growth or learning new things as more

Table 3.2
Importance of Career Goals among Hong Kong Managers

Goal	Hong Kong Firms			U.S. Firms
	Civil Service (n-19)	Service (n-20)	Manufacturing (n-14)	(n-18)
Income	4.2	4.4	4.1	4.1
Prestige	4.2	3.7	3.8	4.1
Power	3.6	3.4	3.2	3.8
Skills	4.1	3.9	3.8	4.8
Creativity	3.7	3.6	3.6	4.6
Fun	3.4	3.8	3.4	3.6
Convenient hours	2.9	3.6	3.5	2.6
Friendship	3.9	3.6	3.5	3.3
Promotions	4.6	4.1	3.9	4.2
Variety	3.5	3.5	3.3	4.0
Autonomy	3.8	3.3	3.9	4.5
Achievement	4.2	3.6	3.8	4.4
Where you live	3.1	2.5	2.9	3.7
Contribution to the organization	4.1	3.5	3.4	4.3
Contribution to the society	3.4	2.8	3.6	3.4
Contribution to your family	3.7	3.0	3.9	4.6
Security	4.0	3.2	3.8	3.4
Comfortable work conditions	3.6	2.8	3.2	3.6
Keep busy	3.3	2.6	2.6	3.0
Fringe benefits	3.9	3.3	3.3	4.0
Meaningful work	4.1	3.3	4.1	4.6
Personal growth	4.4	2.5	3.9	4.6
Well being	3.9	3.0	3.6	4.4

Note: 1 = of little importance, 5 = extremely important.

important. Job security, contribution to society, good relationships, and fun or enjoyment were relatively less important. Convenient working hours was the least important.

In response to an open-ended question about career goals, one manager replied, "We have limited social security here, and my parents were refugees from PRC in 1949, so I need to protect my own life in my retirement and protect the lives of my family." Another said, "Work gives purpose to my life. I have one daughter, and I also need money for her education."

Career Plans.   In general, the respondents had very vague plans or no career plans at all. When asked how long into the future they were thinking about their careers, 75.5 percent of the managers said two to five years. Obviously, people in Hong Kong generally saw the 1997 issue as a limiting effect on their future planning. Ten percent of the respondents from the banking industry had no plans at all, and a further 10 percent to 30 percent had only vague plans. It was surprising to find none of the sample had a very specific plan. The lack of planning was a dominant phenomena among Hong Kong managers. They had no clear plans for their career when they graduated from their professional education programs, and they still did not have plans in mid-career.

Fifteen percent of the respondents in the manufacturing and public sector had never thought about their careers at all. A consistent finding of this study was the clear lack of consideration given to career planning among local managers. Working for a U.S. company did not significantly extend the planning horizon of Hong Kong managers.

Career Blocks and Help.   Respondents were also asked to cite significant factors which had helped or blocked their careers and their attainment of work aspirations. The 1997 transfer was mentioned by a few respondents. The most common primary career blocks mentioned were immediate supervisor, spouse, children, and company policy. In the public sector, slower growth and privatization meant fewer opportunities for promotion. Managers working for U.S. companies cited political events and not being able to speak a foreign language as career blocks. Primary career helps included immediate supervisor, spouse, and company growth. "Nobody else but self help" was mentioned by some respondents. "We are living in a fast moving world. There is the constant need to equip myself with new concepts, to adjust to changes, and to share the knowledge with colleagues in the same company," said one manager.

Managers working for foreign companies also mentioned skill and performance, previous job experience, their degree, broader exposure, and seniority. Hong Kong managers were more likely to think experience would be a help and less likely to believe their immediate supervisor would be a help in their careers. For example one said "My presentation skills, my confidence, and my past career history, that's what will help my career." Another stated, "No one outside will help me, only myself."

One's boss or immediate supervisor was seen as both a help and a block to a chosen career path. It is very easy for a boss to block the career paths of talented employees and to prevent them from developing and realizing their potential. In Chinese-owned companies, owners are prone to repress organizational talent. It is a consequence of not wanting to relinquish power and believing that as owners, they alone should shoulder the responsibilities of the company and therefore make key management decisions (Redding, 1990).

More than 60 percent of the respondents' spouses were employed and working full time. In these dual career families, spouses could help or block the career depending on how the dual career issues are handled. Positive spouse input and family support can be a tremendous help in enhancing career progress. Examples of family support included the following responses: "Most of my time has been spent with my family"; "Kids take up a lot of my time"; and "As a breadwinner, stable income to pay for the bills in the family will impose some pressure on career decisions. A single person will have less constraints in career decisions."

In the structured questions, respondents were asked to rate the amount of influence or control each of several career determinants would have on their careers. The factors most likely to be an influence were (1) the future potential of their jobs, (2) their company's growth potential, (3) their other skills or performance, and (4) the characteristics of their jobs. Teachers, friends, gender, and ethnic or regional origin had the lowest influence over the next job. Chinese managers working for foreign companies claimed political events, their immediate supervisor, friends, and co-workers had relatively little influence. The working relations in these organizations tended to be more impersonal. The number of available jobs, seniority or tenure, previous job experience, and grades or examination scores had much more influence over what their next job might be.

Career Strategies.   Career tactics refer to personal acts aimed primarily at manipulating the informal system that is responsible for career decisions. Respondents were asked about specific tactics they might use or things they might do to advance their own careers. Table 3.3 presents the average score on thirty-six career tactics.

Career tactics ranged from the more proactive strategies of acquiring skills seen as necessary for later career progress, to the more passive strategies of working hard and hoping to be rewarded through later career progress. Almost all of the respondents indicated that they pursued their careers by working hard, doing their current job well, getting more education, and learning more about their business. The next most popular tactics were doing something noticeable, doing better than their peers, gaining rapport with their subordinates, maintaining a network, and conforming to expectations. They were more reluctant to get help from God and leave it to fate or others. Among the least commonly used tactics were threaten to leave or get a second job.

Examples of Hong Kong managers' responses to the open-ended question, What, if anything, are you doing to have the kind of work life or career you want?, included "I am trying to do my job well and I hope to get a reasonable reward"; and "I do my best for my job. I don't ask for what I want. If the company doesn't recognize my efforts I will leave."

OUTCOMES FOR THE ORGANIZATION
AND THE INDIVIDUAL

What recent graduates want in organizations are high salary, fast promotions, and more opportunities to learn and grow on the job. In Hong Kong as well as in other countries, success is most likely to be defined in

Table 3.3
Career Tactics Used by Hong Kong Managers

| Career Tactics | Hong Kong Firms | | | U.S. Firms |
	Civil Service (n=19)	Service (n=20)	Manufacturing (n=14)	(n=18)
Work hard	4.21	4.55	4.21	4.06
Work long hours	3.16	3.70	3.00	3.06
Do your job well	4.37	4.50	4.50	4.78
Do something noticeable	3.16	4.10	3.50	4.06
Do what your boss wants	3.74	4.00	3.64	3.83
Act humble/courteous	3.26	3.65	3.21	3.33
Assertively ask	3.16	3.80	2.79	3.94
Exchange favors	2.63	3.35	3.14	3.00
Threaten to leave	1.42	2.15	1.64	1.67
Develop an action plan	2.63	3.85	2.86	3.67
Seek help from friends	2.72	3.30	2.71	3.33
Show loyalty to the organization	3.37	3.90	3.29	3.67
Show loyalty to your boss	3.37	3.80	3.14	3.39
Learn more about the business	4.21	4.75	4.00	4.50
Get more education	4.37	4.75	4.07	4.18
Gain rapport with subordinates	3.74	4.30	3.79	0.00
Do better than peers	3.84	4.20	3.50	0.00
Become indispensable	2.78	3.40	3.14	0.00
Get important information	3.00	3.35	3.07	0.00
Conform to expectations	3.67	3.65	3.57	0.00
Get help from family	1.79	2.20	2.00	2.06
Get help from God	1.58	1.55	1.50	1.61
Change your family to fit job	1.90	2.60	1.92	2.33
Get a transfer	2.16	2.70	2.29	3.12
Get a job in a new organization	1.95	3.00	2.93	3.35
Get a second job	1.47	2.10	2.07	1.67
Create a new job in the organization	1.74	2.55	2.79	2.00
Get more control of your job	3.22	3.65	3.43	3.56
Change the way you think	2.68	3.15	2.79	3.06
Network	3.39	3.90	3.57	3.83
Start your own company	2.16	2.30	2.43	2.89
Let others recognize you	2.33	3.25	2.93	0.00
Leave it to fate or others	1.84	1.75	2.07	1.33
Tell your boss your career plan	2.21	3.05	2.57	0.00
Get career guidance	1.95	2.85	2.57	0.00

Note: 1 = very unlikely, 5 = very likely.

terms of external factors such as salary, position level, or status. Wealth, education/qualifications, prestige, and popularity are desirable outcomes for the individuals. Others may use their own personal criteria of success with a focus on self-fulfillment, satisfaction, loyalty, and commitment.

Career Choice and Socioeconomic Status

The reasons for joining the civil services depend, to a large extent, on the availability of jobs, the degree or certificate, and to a lesser extent, on the schools managers graduated from. The financial sector has been the most attractive to new graduates, followed by marketing. A declining proportion of graduates is willing to go through professional training such as engineering after graduation. Perhaps these young people have become reluctant to engage in long-term planning and long-term investment in improving their qualifications because of 1997.

In another large social survey in Hong Kong, respondents were asked what criteria determine one's social status. Forty percent of the respondents indicated wealth, 26 percent education, 16 percent contribution to society, 8 percent family background, and 8 percent power (Wong, 1988). When asked about the chances of developing their own careers in the next ten years, the social survey respondents were more cautious and realistic: 20 percent and 15 percent indicated very little chance and little chance respectively; 36 percent believed that their chances would be average, and 22 percent and 7 percent believed that their chances would be great and very good, respectively.

With respect to the perceived best upward-mobility route, two paths emerged. First, it is quite clear that both acquired professional qualifications and starting one's own business were most favored, chosen by 39 percent and 41 percent of the respondents, respectively. The second track was finding a job with good promotion prospects (Wong, 1988).

The outcomes of career planning from both individual and organizational perspectives will be reflected in effectiveness, satisfaction, and commitment. In general, the respondents claimed that work was important in their lives. They were quite successful and satisfied with their lives and career goals. To a varying degree, they have just met their career expectations.

Career Success.   Career success as described by one respondent from the public sector in the study is "being respected by the public, making a contribution to the community, and having a reasonably comfortable lifestyle." Another respondent put it this way, "Career success to me means how well prepared is one to absorb responsibility, to make decision at major issues and always ready to lead your staff towards the organization goal." The overall success was measured by one single self-reported question, "How likely are you to achieve success in your career?" The answer ranged from 0 percent to 100 percent chance, with 60 percent of bank employees and 70 percent of manufacturing employees reporting moderate success.

Perceived career success was significantly correlated with the career tactics of using assertiveness, having an action plan, being willing to learn more about business, getting more information, and developing a positive relationship with peers and subordinates. The proactive strategies of "working hard and acquiring qualifications" are the most frequently mentioned career tactics leading to career success. Respondents believed people need continual development in order to succeed in a rapidly changing Hong Kong environment. The number of promotions was correlated with doing something noticeable, gaining recognition, and assertiveness. There seems to be a connection between ingratiation and promotion in Hong Kong. Career success may not be restricted to upward movement or advancement. Laterality and centrality are both patterns of career achievement that people actually pursue. However, it is not common for local Chinese companies to make use of job enlargement.

Career Satisfaction. In assessing the overall job satisfaction of groups of public employees, Burns (1984) tried to investigate whether those determinants of satisfaction, such as age, tenure, pay, occupational level, and education were related to job satisfaction in the civil service in Hong Kong. Results showed that satisfaction was positively related to age, rank, tenure, pay, and education. He believes these results could be explained by the selection effect. The longer a worker stayed on the job, the more likely it was that he or she would be satisfied. The more dissatisfied civil servants would have left the government after joining for a few years when they were younger. On the whole, the respondents reported moderate career satisfaction.

In this study, responses to the open-ended question, In general, how do you feel about your career so far?, were quite positive—"so far so good." If the respondents were given an opportunity to start all over again, the majority of them would pick the same occupation. A few of them would like to change. One respondent in the banking sector claimed, "I would rather work for the property development industry." Another respondent said, "I would like to start my own business. It offers a much better opportunity to earn a fortune."

Generic life satisfaction was measured by the questions, In general, how satisfied are you with meeting your career goals so far in your life?, and In general, how satisfied are you with your life? The mean scores for service, manufacturing, and civil servants were 3.35, 3.2, and 3.63, respectively; 69.8 percent of the respondents reported being moderately satisfied with self-perceived career success; 86.8 percent with their career; 81.6 percent with their life in general.

In the structured questions, job satisfaction was measured by twenty-three items (using a five-point scale) including satisfaction with income, benefits, power, contribution, growth, and general well being (see Table 3.4). Organizational satisfaction was emphasized rather than job satisfaction because a career extends beyond one job in most cases. The respondents were particularly satisfied with job security, income, and working conditions and less satisfied with power and influence and fun or enjoyment.

Table 3.4
Career Satisfaction

Satisfaction	Hong Kong Firms			U.S. Firms
	Civil Service (n-19)	Service (n-20)	Manufacturing (n-14)	(n-18)
Income	3.3	3.4	3.1	3.5
Prestige	2.9	3.6	2.8	3.6
Power	2.8	3.5	2.5	3.5
Skills	2.9	3.7	3.2	3.9
Creativity	2.9	3.5	2.7	3.6
Fun	2.7	3.3	3.0	3.2
Convenient hours	3.5	3.4	2.5	3.1
Friendship	2.9	3.5	2.9	3.2
Promotions	2.8	3.7	3.2	3.6
Variety	2.8	3.1	3.2	3.8
Autonomy	3.1	3.5	2.9	3.9
Achievement	3.1	3.5	3.3	4.1
Where you live	3.2	3.4	3.5	3.6
Contribution to the organization	2.9	3.5	3.5	4.2
Contribution to the society	3.1	3.0	3.4	2.7
Contribution to your family	3.1	3.3	3.3	3.4
Security	3.9	3.7	2.8	3.5
Comfortable work condition	3.4	3.5	2.5	3.1
Keep busy	3.1	3.4	3.0	3.5
Fringe benefits	3.2	3.4	2.7	2.8
Meaningful work	2.9	3.4	2.9	3.7
Personal growth	2.9	3.5	3.1	3.8
Well being	3.0	3.4	2.9	3.7

Note: 1 = very dissatisfied, 5 = very satisfied.

The respondents from the banking industry generally were more satisfied than the other two groups because it is generally considered prestigious to work in a bank. Compared with the private sector employees, the civil servants were more satisfied with job security and convenient working hours. Civil servants generally have more stable and secure working conditions and less overtime work.

Employees of U.S. companies were generally more satisfied with achievement of challenge, contributing to the company, power and influence, advancement or promotion, and growth or learning. American multinational firms usually offer better salary and fringe benefits and more challenge than domestic Hong Kong firms.

In the present study, career satisfaction was correlated with the career tactics of asking for help, loyalty to organization and boss, and more education and learning more about business. The career tactics of conforming to the boss's expectation and organizational practices produce positive results. Having a career which met the employee's expectations correlated with showing loyalty, getting more learning and education, having a career plan, and developing a positive relationship with subordinates.

Research results indicate that levels of satisfaction varied across departments and across the organizational hierarchy. The level of satisfaction was relatively higher among senior professionals than among nonprofessionals or generalists. These better educated professionals also received relatively higher salaries. Satisfaction among the lower level of employees, especially among the rank-and-file disciplined officers, was the lowest. Hong Kong civil servants found intrinsic aspects of their work and relations with their co-workers most satisfying. The most prominent source of dissatisfaction identified was government promotion policies and practices.

Organization Commitment and Intent to Stay.   High turnover rates and employee retention were cited as the most critical tasks by human resources managers. For the individual, changing jobs may realize a short-term gain. However, frequently job hopping may create a lot of problems for the organization in maintaining a stable workforce. An earlier study (Cheek-Milby, 1988) showed that approximately one in five of a sample of forty-four civil servants plan to emigrate. Two-thirds of the respondents were determined to stay in the civil service after 1997. Those who were thinking about leaving cited a number of reasons, the predominant being retirement (24%), followed by emigration (21%), fear of political interference (18%), better chance of promotion (16%), and better pay (16%).

In the present study, intent to stay was measured by the question, How long do you expect to continue working for this organization? About half (47.4%) of the civil servants did not answer this question. They were very uncertain about their futures. Among those who responded, half of them indicated that they could stay for ten years; that is, beyond 1997. The average expected organizational tenure for Hong Kong managers in other economic sectors was 8.3 years. Fifty percent of them indicated that they would stay less than five years. The 1997 issue cast some doubt on the future of Hong Kong. Twenty-one percent of the managers reported that they would leave the company in less than five years. Changing jobs had some negative impact on managers' careers in terms of satisfaction, expectation, and pay level.

The measure for organization commitment, a three-item scale, was derived from Meyer and Allen (1984) (i.e., This organization means a lot to me, I am not part of this organizational family, and I do not belong to this organization). Organization commitment was significantly correlated with perceptions that the organization used influence tactics of "treats me like a family" and "shares organization information." Working in an organization that gives good fringe benefits, shows appreciation, offers future opportunities, offers good training, has an organization culture/mission, and rewards goals achieved was also correlated with higher organization commitment. These practices are more commonly used in multinational corporations. That is one reason why Chinese managers working for U.S. subsidiaries were more satisfied and committed.

Commitment was significantly related to using individual career tactics such as asking powerful people for help, seeking help from friends and family, changing the way you think, developing rapport with subordinates, and changing family plans to fit the job. Intent to stay was significantly positively correlated with use of individual career tactics such as getting help from God and getting a transfer but negatively correlated with conforming to expectations and getting a job in a new organization.

Limitations

It is necessary to address certain limitations of the present study. The present study relied on self-reported data from a small sample of Chinese managers. It is possible that self-report data biased the relationships observed. Another point worth mentioning is the lack of longitudinal data on career movement. It takes many years to achieve career success. This study observed a relatively small sample of Hong Kong Chinese managers that may not be readily generalized to all managers in Hong Kong and used retrospective accounts to gain information about how careers changed across time. Despite these shortcomings, it is still possible to make some tentative recommendations and important observations about the career attitudes, beliefs, and organizational career development practices among Hong Kong companies.

IMPLICATIONS FOR CAREER MANAGEMENT AND DEVELOPMENT

Career development programs can benefit both the individual and the organization. Thus it is necessary for both individuals and organizations to make an effort to promote career development. Contrary to the traditional thinking that it is important to be very clear about desired career goals, the findings of this study indicate that career planning was not generally used by the respondents in this study. It seems that career planning and development were not an important tool for the local Chinese managers. Perhaps when there are many jobs available, they do not see the urgent need to plan. Hong Kong is in a state of transition, and people tend to be very short-sighted. Fresh graduates stay at their first job for a short time and show little loyalty or commitment toward the company or their boss. The "get what you can while you can" attitude is common.

The research findings in this study have considerable implications for developing local managers. The efficiency of planning has been established in the area of corporate strategy, and planning has been advocated for years by career guidance personnel and vocational counselors. One of the most interesting areas for further work is to seek a more detailed explanation for why career planning is not often done and whether there is anything particular to the Hong Kong political situation or cultural heritage that makes it difficult to plan, important to plan, or useless to plan.

Implications for the Society

Future direction and policies should include continuous development of Hong Kong's most valuable human resources in the highly competitive global economy. Industrial/vocational training schemes, centers of education excellence in universities and polytechnics, a flexible labor market policy to address shortages, and a strategy to reduce emigration of key personnel from Hong Kong and to increase immigration of key personnel are all necessary policies if Hong Kong is to continue to be one of the Four Dragons.

The changes in Hong Kong after 1997 are enormous in many different aspects. Managers must learn to adapt to new regulations, yet they should be active in learning how to create opportunities. They will have to be especially flexible in the next decade to acquaint themselves with PRC's way of doing business.

Implications for the Organization

Chinese managers in Hong Kong organizations, to a large extent, showed a varied pattern of organization commitment. Family ties are important in Chinese societies. The tendency to employ close relatives in family businesses helps to ensure that control and wealth are kept in the family. Nonfamily members have limited opportunity for progress through the ranks to top managerial positions. Such restricted career opportunity affects the managers' satisfaction with these human resources practices, which in turn influences their commitment to stay in the same company to pursue their careers.

Most employers preferred loyal and committed employees. In 1989, a survey of personnel management practices in 361 Hong Kong companies revealed that only 37 percent provided management development to their staff. These were mostly larger companies as well as multinational corporations (Kirkbride & Tang, 1989). The majority of these Chinese organizations, even the larger ones, had not done enough to develop a more motivated, committed, and high caliber workforce. U.S. companies operating in Hong Kong did not differ too much from local companies. However, Chinese managers working in U.S. companies were generally more satisfied. Most people feel it is prestigious to work in U.S. subsidiaries. These organizations inherited some Western management practices and offer better salary and benefits. Also, there may be chances to work in overseas branches, or the U.S. companies may sponsor some of their local employees to get a U.S. passport.

What were the respondents' views on career development? Despite the managers' general acceptance and agreement on the importance of career development, the present study shows that a wide gap exists between what managers believe and what they actually practice. To a large extent, systematic career planning and development is not widely practiced in these local Chinese companies. As a result, these companies may not be able to recruit and retain the best employees in a tight labor market situation. The difficulties of employee retention in a tight labor market, together with the rising labor cost, are developing signs of the need for increased effort on the part of organizations to use human resources more effectively. Chinese companies may need to take career planning and development more seriously in order to begin to address these problems.

Implications for the Individual

The findings of this study suggest that individuals may need to be more proactive in taking charge of their careers. The traditional tactics of working hard, conforming to expectations, getting help from family and friends, or threatening to leave had no significant relationship to feelings of career success. Also, the tactics of getting a new job and leaving it to fate or others had a negative relationship to perceived career success.

One of the most important career strategies Hong Kong workers used was to acquire more training. The importance of continuing development was also stressed. In a rapidly changing business world, the traditional practices of simply working hard and doing the job well are nota enough. Findings indicate that managers need to act more assertively, develop action plans and networks, get important information, and learn more about the business. The finding in this study confirmed Tam's (1990) observation that the entrepreneurial development system in Hong Kong is different from the way managers are trained in the Western countries. Chinese managers were not trained; they developed themselves experientially and continually throughout their lives. Career and management development programs are likely to be well received by employees in Hong Kong and have great potential for success. The pursuit of education is an important cultural value among the Chinese people. Commitment to educating oneself in order to improve one's career prospects is more deeply rooted in Hong Kong than in many Western countries. Employees are more prepared to spend evenings studying or taking classes than employees in the West and are not dependant upon their companies for training (Redding, Wong, Tam, & Yeung, 1986). If organizations were to address this desire by offering career-related training, more could be done to integrate employees' personal goals and career activities with the organizational goals.

In sum, the present study is a preliminary investigation in exploring the complex interaction of some prominent determinants of career patterns. These is still room for improvement. There definitely is a need for future studies in the pursuit of a more comprehensive understanding of how careers progress in Hong Kong organizations.

REFERENCES

Bank Training Board. (1992). *1992 manpower survey report on the banking industry*. Hong Kong: Vocational Training Council.

Burns, J. P. (1984). Job satisfaction in the Hong Kong civil service. In I. Scott & J. P. Burns (Eds.), *The Hong Kong civil service: Personnel policies and practices* (pp. 37–53). Hong Kong: Oxford University Press.

Census and Statistics Department. (1995). *Census Statistics*. Hong Kong: Government Printer.

Cheek-Milby, K. (1988). Identifying the issues. In I. Scott & J. P. Burns (Eds.), *The Hong Kong civil service and its future* (pp. 109–130). Hong Kong: Oxford University Press.

Cheng, J. Y. S. (1992). Values and attitudes of the Hong Kong community. In P. C. K. Kwong (Ed.), *Hong Kong trends 1989–1992: Index to other Hong Kong reports* (pp. 62–80). Hong Kong: Chinese University Press.

Chow, I. H. S. (1988). Work related values of middle managers in the private and public sectors. *Proceedings of the Academy of International Business Southeast Asia Regional Conference* (pp. A14–25). Bangkok, Thailand: Human Resources Institute, Thammasat University.

Chow, I. H. S. (1990). An empirical assessment of organizational commitment among local employees. *Human Resources Journal*, 6(1), 32–38.

Cooper, T. L., & Lui, T. L. (1990, May/June). Democracy and administrative state: The case of Hong Kong. *Public Administrative Review*, 332–344.

Gutteridge, T. (1988). Organizational career development systems: The state of the practice. In D. Hall (Ed.), *Career development in organizations* (pp. 50–94). San Francisco: Jossey-Bass.

Hackman, J. R., & Oldham, G. R. (1976). Motivation through design of work: Test of a theory. *Organizational Behavior and Human Performance, 16*, 250–279.

Hofstede, G. (1980). *Culture's consequences*. Beverly Hills, CA: Sage.

Hong Kong Annual Report. (1990, 1992, 1995, 1996). Hong Kong Government Printer.

Hong Kong Industrial Relations Association. (1991). *Pay level survey for the manu-facturing sector*. Hong Kong: The Association.

Kipnis, D., Schmidt, S., & Wilkinson, I. (1980). Intra-organizational influence tactics: Explorations in getting one's way. *Journal of Applied Psychology, 65*, 440–452.

Kirkbride, P. S., & Tang, F.Y.S. (1989). *The present state of personnel management in Hong Kong*. Vocational Training Council, Hong Kong Government Printer.

Kwong, P. C. C. (1992). *Hong Kong trends 1989–92*. Hong Kong: Chinese University Press.

Liu, T. L. (1992). Work and work value. In S. K. Lau, M. K. Lee, P. S. Wan, & S. Wong (Eds.), *Indicators of social development, Hong Kong 1992* (pp. 105–127). Hong Kong: Hong Kong Institute of Asian-Pacific Studies, Chinese University of Hong Kong.

Management Development Center of Hong Kong. (1988). *The first interim report on a study of the in-company management development practice of Hong Kong companies*. Hong Kong: Vocational Training Council.

Meyer, J., & Allen, N. (1984). Testing the side bet theory of organizational com-mitment: Some methodological considerations. *Journal of Applied Psychol-ogy, 69*, 372–378.

Mobley, W. H., Griffith, R. W., Hand, N. H., & Meglino, B. M. (1979). Review and conceptual analysis of the employee turnover process. *Psychological Bulletin, 86*, 493–522.

Redding, S. G., Wong, G. Y. Y., Tam, S. K. W., & Yeung, A. K. O. (1986). *Manage-ment practices in Hong Kong*. Mong Kwok Ping Data Bank Working Paper. University of Hong Kong.

Redding, S. G. (1990). *The spirit of Chinese capitalism*. New York: Walter de Gruyter.

Shenkar, O., & Ronen, S. (1987). Structure and importance of work goals among managers in the People's Republic of China. *Academy of Management Journal, 30*(3), 564–576.

Tam, S. (1990). Centrifugal versus centripetal growth process: Contrasting ideal types from conceptualizing the development patterns of Chinese and Japa-nese firms. In S. Clegg, & S. G. Redding (Eds.), *Capitalism in contrasting cultures* (pp. 153–183). New York: Walter de Gruyter.

Wong, C. S. (1992). Organizational commitment and job characteristics: Some exploratory evidence in Hong Kong. *Hong Kong Journal of Business Man-agement, 9*, 45–57.

Wong, T. W. P. (1988). Inequality, satisfaction, and mobility. In S. K. Lau, M. K. Lee, P. S. Wan, & S. Wong (Eds.), *Indicators of social development: Hong Kong* (p. 164). Hong Kong Government Printer.

Wong, T. W. P. (1990). Training and career development for the hospitality in-dustry. *Hong Kong Manager, 26*(2), 22–23.

Yeh, R. S. (1989). On Hofstede's treatment of Chinese and Japanese values. *Asia Pacific Journal of Management, 6*(1), 149–160.

CHAPTER FOUR

Careers of Managers in Taiwan

Tai-Kuang Peng

This chapter explores the organizational career management practices and managers' career planning patterns in Taiwan. The general development of career perceptions in a country has much to do with its cultural, societal, and historical background. Therefore, we need to identify the factors affecting the career decisions of Taiwanese managers. Using many related studies, published statistics, and the interviews of 120 managers in seven organizations, this chapter creates a picture of careers of the managerial workforce in the Chinese society of Taiwan. The interviewed respondents' answers describe the career beliefs, strategies, and career paths of individual managers participating in the study as well as the practices and norms of their employing organizations. Differences between respondents working for U.S. and Taiwanese firms also are explored.

NATIONAL CONTEXT

Though Taiwan enjoys world fame for its "economic miracle," most people in other regions have only a vague impression of where Taiwan is and what it is like. The brief introduction below may clarify the picture and provide a context for career patterns of Taiwanese managers.

Taiwan Yesterday and Today

Taiwan is a leaf-shaped island straddling the tropic of Cancer, about 200 kilometers (120 miles) off the eastern shore of the Chinese mainland.

Located in the East China sea, Taiwan is midway between Japan and Korea to the north and Hong Kong and the Philippines to the south. With a land area of 36,000 square kilometers (13,900 square miles), the island is close to the size of the Netherlands.

In 1895, Taiwan was ceded to Japan in the Sino-Japanese War. After fifty years of colonial Japanese rule, it was restored to Nationalist Chinese control by the end of World War II. In 1949, President Chiang Kai-Shek led his 2 million troops and followers across the Taiwan Straits. After an arduous twenty-year period, Taiwan now enjoys prosperity and modern development.

The majority of Taiwan's Chinese populace traces its ancestry back to the Fukien province in mainland China. In addition, about 323,000 ethnic aborigines live in remote mountain villages (Ministry of Transportation & Communications, 1991). By the end of May 1996, the population of Taiwan was nearly 21.4 million, with the proportion of males to females being 1.06 to 1. With such a large population on a small island, Taiwan is one of the most densely populated pieces of land on earth. For instance, about 2.7 million people live in the capital city of Taipei, which covers an area of about 272 square kilometers (105 square miles), making its population density 9,828 persons per square kilometer. Viewed from another angle, such a bounty in human resources has been the basis of Taiwan's economic development (Ministry of Interior, 1993).

Figures released from many sources document Taiwan's rapid growth. According to statistics from the International Monetary Foundation (IMF) and the World Bank, the average per capita gross national product (GNP) of Taiwan was US$8,788 in 1991, leaping from 31st in 1985 to 25th in 1991, larger than three-fourths of the nations in the United Nations (IMF, 1994; Nixon, 1994). With a foreign exchange reserve of more than US$90 billion, it ranks as the second wealthiest nation in Asia.

However, Taiwan is not rich in natural raw materials. This makes it essential for Taiwan to export a large amount of manufactured goods to survive. The United States and Japan are its two most important trade partners, and Germany is its most important trade partner in Europe. In 1993, Taiwan ranked as the fourteenth biggest trading country in the world, about the same as the previous few years.

Flush with profits, Taiwan has begun spending heavily on giant infrastructure projects to modernize its economy and build the foundation for future growth. Taiwan is launching a US$300 billion six-year development plan that focuses on the construction of highways, subways, and power plants. The development plan is expected to raise annual per capita GNP to US$14,000 by 1996, and figures released recently show that the goal is well underway: per capita GNP was $11,597 in 1994 and $12,439 in 1995, respectively (Directorate-General of Budget, 1996).

The economic boom has created a sizable and fast growing middle class. In general, the distribution of wealth in Taiwan is even, but the gap between the rich and poor has been getting larger in recent years. Two national surveys (1992 and 1993) conducted by Directorate-General of Budget, Accounting and Statistics, Executive Yuan revealed that the total wealth of the richest 20 percent of families was 16.8 times that of the poorest 20 percent families in 1991, and that the average household income of the richest 20 percent was about 5.2 times of that of the poorest 20 percent of families in 1992. Furthermore, five big family-run business groups, offering 140,000 job opportunities in total, account for 5 percent of Taiwan's overall wealth and about 10 percent of Taiwan's GNP (Sheen, 1993).

In spite of Taiwan's economic achievements, it has formal diplomatic relationships with few countries for political reasons, though many countries engage in various cultural and economic activities unofficially. At present, only thirty nations in the world recognize the People's Republic of China. In recent years, Taiwan has been active in the attempt to win recognition. In 1991, Taiwan became a member of the Asia-Pacific Economic Cooperation Forum (APEC). Currently, it is making great efforts to join the World Trade Organization (WTO) and to make a comeback to the United Nations.

Changing Economy and Society

As foreign trade in Taiwan moved from the stage of rapid growth to stable development, Taiwan began shedding slow-growth industries such as textiles and steel and shifted from producing consumer goods into the manufacture of higher-value-added products such as computers. In 1987, the government ended martial law. As a result, the New Taiwan dollar (NT$) greatly appreciated. This also contributed to the change in industry structure. In 1993, heavy industry accounted for 61.45 percent of overall manufacturing. In 1993, the top 500 companies engaged in service accounted for 55.9 percent of the total GDP, far more than the 40.6 percent contributed by the top 500 manufacturing companies. This was the first time the GDP of service industries exceeded that of manufacturing. Furthermore, the service sector contribution to the GDP is growing at the fast pace of 11.56 percent, while that of manufacturing is growing at only 2.2 percent per year.

From the early stage of using low-wage labor to manufacture low-quality products, to its present status as the leading exporter of high-tech products such as computer chips and accessories, modern Taiwan has come a long way by conscientiously adapting to market trends. Taiwan has fully entered the service-oriented era (Liu, 1994; Ministry of Economic Affairs, 1994).

The shift in industrial structure also has affected employment opportunities. In the year 1987, about 35 percent of the working population worked in the manufacturing sector, and 42 percent worked in services. However, by early 1996, only 26.9 percent remained employed in manufacturing, and the percentage of people working in the service sector had risen to 51.7 percent (Council of Labor Affairs, 1996).

The change in industry structure is further evidenced by the average salary of the professions. In general, people working in service industries earn much more than those in manufacturing. The average monthly salary in the period of January to July 1993, showed that the four best-paid professions belonged to service industries: telecommunication—US$2,960; business consulting—US$2,800; electricity supply and harbor transportation—US$2,520; finance (especially foreign banks)—US$2,480. On the other hand, the average monthly earnings of each employee in the manufacturing industry was only US$1,189 (Directorate of Statistics, 1993).

Unions have played an important role in labor employment since martial law ended. Low-echelon laborers have been the creators of Taiwan's economic miracle, but in terms of the distribution of economic achievement and political participation, they have always been an underprivileged group. In recent years, labor unions have been very active. However, due to the unique political and historical background of Taiwan, unions have experienced conflict with management and government (Council of Labor Affairs, 1992). In the first quarter of 1996, there were 1,193 industrial unions, 2,393 craft unions, and 62 nationwide or regional federations of unions, with a total membership of 3,080,000 and an organization rate of 45.7 percent (Council of Labor Affairs, 1996). Politically speaking, from an early authoritarian tradition to political liberalization and economic maturity, Taiwan has experienced an air of increased openness in the society.

Tomorrow's Challenges and Opportunities

Although it maintains an annual growth rate of 6 to 7 percent, Taiwan is not without problems. The low-wage social structure and high savings rate that once helped create economic success have changed. The average private consumption rate has increased sharply. By the first quarter of 1996, the savings rate was only 20.49 percent, down about 15 percent from the peak period in 1987. In addition, the strong collective ethic that has played a crucial role in Taiwan's development is also diminishing.

Taiwan's economy will have to overcome several challenges to continue to expand. In the 1970s, Taiwan was listed as one of the four Little Dragons. Recently the list has been extended to become the Super Seven. Newcomers like Vietnam and the PRC are important competitors (Shapiro, 1993).

The vast market of mainland China is seen as an undeveloped land with great potential. Being the sixth biggest trade partner of mainland China, Taiwan has become PRC's most important foreign investor (China Daily, 1996). The trade between the two is enormous—most is thinly disguised by going through Hong Kong. According to a briefing on the foreign investments of Taiwanese enterprises by the Ministry of Economic Affairs (1994), the number of manufacturing enterprises in Taiwan making investments on mainland China was about 47 percent of the total foreign investment in 1993, a 26 percent increase of the previous year. Furthermore, the same source revealed that more than 50 percent of the domestic companies, both in number and amount, are willing to invest on mainland China in the three years ahead. In addition to competition from mainland China and other rapidly developing economies, domestic protectionism is another threat. Sheltered industries are being forced to face keen competition from Taiwan's world trade liberation.

National Employment and Career Behavior

The human resources of Taiwan are also changing in structure. The average age is increasing at an annual rate of 0.35 years. Taiwan now has passed Japan as the fastest aging nation in the world. An aging population structure will place a heavy burden on social welfare expenditures in the foreseeable future (Council for Economic Development and Planning, 1992).

The problem of hidden unemployment is also noteworthy. By the end of May, 1996, potential workers over the age of fifteen constituted 76.6 percent of the total population, and the actual workforce numbered 9.3 million. However, it is estimated that 32.4 percent of the employed population is underemployed, meaning their position and expertise do not match or they are simply underpaid.

Although the unemployment rate in Taiwan is remarkably low compared with most Western countries, it has steadily increased, and that of highly educated people is perceived as relatively high. For the past nine years, the unemployment rates have remained below 2 percent. The figure was 1.56 percent in 1994 and 1.79 percent for 1995, respectively; however, the rate had risen to 2.35 percent by May 1996, and is still going up. Officials in the Council for Economic Development and Planning (1993) revealed that the current job market in Taiwan features "excessive highly-educated human resources, and insufficient low-echelon workers." Taking 1992 as an example, the overall unemployment rate was 1.5 percent. But the rate for university graduates and above was 2.3 percent; for college graduates, 2.1 percent; for junior middle school graduates (seventh to ninth grades) 1.5 percent; and for grade school graduates (first to sixth) 0.5 percent.

Meanwhile, the labor force participation rate (LFP) has been getting lower by the year and the figure is still dropping. The LFP has fallen from 60.9 percent in 1987 to 59 percent in 1993, far lower than 66 percent in the U.S. and 64 percent in Japan for the same year. The LFP rate was 58.28 percent for the month of May, 1996 (Council of Labor Affairs, 1996).

Two main reasons account for the decline in the proportion of potential workers who join the actual workforce. First, as living standards rise, people value recreation and leisure more than work. As an example, travel and tourism has become one of the fastest growing industries in Taiwan. Another reason is closely associated with the important role education plays in Chinese society. Young people in Taiwan tend to spend an increased number of years in advanced studies, and this causes a delay in entering the job market. For example, in 1992 the labor force participation rate for university graduates was 63.4 percent, about 10 percent lower than that of college graduates. In general, a college student spends about two to three years beyond high school to obtain a certificate or diploma, while it takes at least four years for a university student to obtain a bachelor's degree. Thus, changing the idea that more diplomas are always needed and making effective use of the considerable number of potential workers has become a big challenge for the human resources planning authorities of Taiwan.

Another noteworthy phenomenon is the low labor force participation rate for women. In 1995, the LFP rate for females was only 45.5 percent, and that of males was 72.1 percent. This rate is influenced by many factors, including differences in age, education level, family income, the husband's attitude toward a working wife, and the age of children.

One study (Council of Labor Affairs, 1993) on the participation rate of women in Taiwan provides several interesting explanations by comparing Taiwanese women to those in the Western countries. First, women in Taiwan generally are more attached to marriage and family. As it is not easy to get jobs that balance work and family well, most women would sacrifice their own careers for their husband and children when choices have to be made. Thus, many women take "quitting my job after getting married" for granted. It was reported that from 1979 to 1990 about one-third of Taiwanese women who had a job before marriage quit after they got married. More quit after giving birth, as they tend to raise children by themselves instead of taking them to child care centers. Living customs and diet habits are also an influencing factor. Taiwanese women devote much more time to household maintenance and meals than women in Western countries.

Moreover, the job market information system is not yet fully active and open in Taiwan. When women consider going to work after years at home after the children are all grown, they rarely find a suitable job, due to lack of professional assistance, expertise, and mental preparedness. Taking these factors into account, the figures of labor participation rates for married women in Taiwan become self-explanatory: LFP of women with no children is 60.5 percent; with children under six years old it is 44.4 percent; with children six to seventeen years old it is 52.5 percent; with children over eighteen years old it is 32 percent (Council for Economic Development and Planning, 1991).

As public and private employment service offices are unavailable, major ways of looking for jobs in Taiwan are through an introduction by relatives and friends or through newspapers and electronic media. A national report commissioned by the Council of Labor Affairs indicated that 76.9 percent of people got their jobs through enterprise advertisements in mass media or newspapers, 74.9 percent through the introduction of relatives and friends, 28 percent through the arrangement of schools, 21.2 percent through governmental employment services; only 11 percent of jobs were obtained through private employment services (Shy, 1992).

The Educational System

Society in Taiwan is deeply influenced by Confucian thought. The priority in choosing a profession has always been scholar, farmer, laborer, and businessman, in that order. Business was always listed last among the four major professions. Nowadays, with the world trend becoming economy-oriented, the preferences have not been as distinct, but with the deep-rooted belief of "study is supreme among all things" and the active support of the government, higher education is still the primary pursuit of many youngsters throughout childhood and young adulthood.

Taiwan has adopted a nine-year compulsory education policy, and this is expected to be extended to twelve years in the near future. The national joint college entrance examination used to be called a "narrow gate," but in recent years, the gate has been broadened to accommodate almost half of the applicants each year.

In previous years, higher education meant higher status and better paying jobs. Although highly educated people are still more prestigious in general, it seems that the logic of education procuring good jobs has failed. Job seekers with high educational degrees find that the job market is getting more and more unwelcome. Though job vacancies are plentiful, the average demand-to-supply ratio for college graduates is 0.95, but for university graduates and above the ratio is less than 0.60.

The major reason for the oversupply of the highly educated is that economic development cannot keep up with the educational system, which produces an increasing number of bachelors, masters, and Ph.D. recipients each year. On the other hand, the global recession is also an important factor. The number of returning overseas scholars who once found good job offers abroad has multiplied in recent years. The reversed brain drain makes a greater imbalance in the supply/demand ratio of educated workers.

National Career Beliefs

Career goals and values of Taiwanese society are revealed in several ways, including surveys of employer choice and desirable working conditions. In a survey of entry-level college graduates, income was only sixth among the reasons they chose a particular firm (Jan, 1992). The most highly valued factors in choosing a position were (1) personal interests (15.1%); (2) chance for promotion and development (13.7%); (3) job security (13.3%); (4) opportunity for further study and learning (12.1%); and (5) good and complete welfare benefits (10.7%).

However, in the national Work Experience Survey, which included all domestic workers who were currently employed and willing to work in the following year, the order of priority of preferred working conditions was different (Council of Labor Affairs, 1993). This report indicated that 37 percent of respondents thought income was the most important consideration, job security was second (17%), and welfare and days off were third (10%). Among the rest, the order by importance was job location, work hours, work safety and hygiene, the chance to use expertise, and a sound personnel system. In all, training and education opportunities and harmonious labor–management relationships were considered least important.

Moreover, the survey found that women considered location near home and shorter work time to be very important, while men more highly valued salary and job safety. On the other hand, blue-collar workers tended to value more tangible conditions such as income, work hours, security, and location, while white-collar workers valued more personnel and welfare systems, the use of their expertise, training and education opportunities offered, and labor–management relationships.

Another strong work value in Taiwan is ownership of a business (Gen, 1992). Taiwan's economy consists mostly of medium and small enterprises. According to the statistics of the Ministry of Economic Affairs (Central Daily, 1994), there were more than 901,000 medium and small enterprises by the end of 1993, an increase of about 30,000 from 1992. These enterprises account for 96.5 percent of the total number of Taiwanese enterprises, providing 78.7 percent of the national employment opportunities. It is estimated that there are 2.5 CEOs for every 100 persons. Some may wonder how these CEOs are produced: Actually, the reason most CEOs in Taiwan reach their position today is that they are self-employed entrepreneurs. The survey made by *Management Monthly* (Jan, 1992) found that the second most popular reason for employees leaving the company was entrepreneurship (the first reason being low salary, the third being lack of chance for promotion).

A main reason for this phenomenon may be the proverb literally translated as, "It is better to be the head of a chicken than the tail of an ox." This adage explains people's mentality that they would rather have a low but independent position than a high but controlled one. Actually, the reasons CEOs said they pursued entrepreneurship included having (1) full use of expertise and ability (35.2%); (2) not being controlled by others (32.2%); and (3) a better chance of making money (21.3%) (Jan, 1992).

A 1992 survey of general managers (GM) in Taiwan had a similar result (Shin Yih Cultural Foundation, 1993). Among the 101 usable questionnaires, it was found that a great majority of GM respondents were produced because they started their own business. For example, for the question, How was a GM created? the answers were (1) by initiating own business (62.5%); (2) by being promoted from within (22.5%); (3) through family relationships (9.5%); and (4) by corporate raiding (4.7%).

However, in the highly competitive environment of Taiwan, being a CEO is no easy job. Statistics show that more than 48,000 profit-seeking enterprises went out of business in 1992, about 64 percent more than the previous year. Realizing that "you are either going forward or backward," most CEOs are making efforts to enrich their knowledge of management. A survey reported the three means of self-development used most were reading related books, taking management-related courses offered by consulting services (which are blooming in Taiwan nowadays), and engaging in short-term study abroad (Gen, 1992).

ORGANIZATIONAL CAREER MANAGEMENT

Family business is typical of the enterprises in Taiwan, but it is definitely not the only type of business. In a study titled "Organization Patterns and Employees' Morale in Taiwan," Hwang (1983) divided Taiwanese enterprises into three major categories: private business ruled by systems (i.e., enterprises adopting Western management systems and practices); family business ruled by owners; and foreign-invested companies.

Lack of formal authorization and long-term planning, especially about careers, used to be a feature of family enterprises, but the situation is changing gradually. In 1991, Shih (1991) conducted a survey on the current human resources practice in manufacturing enterprises in Taiwan. Among the top 500 manufacturing firms in 1992, questionnaires were sent to 282 companies with at least 500 employees. In the 117 questionnaires returned, 57 percent claimed to already have a career planning system or to have put one into practice.

In these large companies, most managers are promoted from within, especially those at senior levels. The survey also indicated that the main criteria for promoting managers are: (1) good character and work attitudes; (2) leadership and managing ability; and (3) expertise and talent (Shih, 1991).

In a similar survey on enterprise requirements and recruitment of employees, the most valuable considerations for hiring the managers were (1) expertise; (2) good character; (3) managing ability; and (4) communication skills (Liao, 1992).

For career planning practices to succeed, human resources managers suggested the following requirements: (1) participation of top management; (2) sound personnel systems and lateral systems, as well as clear job descriptions; and (3) consensus of all the departments and employees (Shih, 1991). Two major conclusions can be reached from these surveys. First, the number of Taiwanese firms where a career planning system has been put into practice is approaching that of foreign countries. Second, companies with career planning systems have a relatively low and stable turnover rate.

We now have a broad picture of the current cultural context and general career management practices in Taiwan. In comparison, the specific career management practices of each organization and of the managers interviewed in the present study are described in the following sections.

Organizational Career Management of Study Firms

Organization A is one of the leading manufacturing enterprises in Taiwan, hiring 12,000 employees in total. The head office is located in Taipei, and the organization participating in the present study is its Kaohsiung branch. As a well-established company, its mission statement and management philosophy are clearly stated.

The career paths also are clearly drawn in organization A. Most people start as engineers and get the chance of being promoted to junior managers only after working for ten to twelve years. The average age of the employees is 39.2 years, and the majority are male. The average service time in the company is fourteen years, and most employees intend to stay until retirement. However, the average number of promotions is only 2.4 times, and usually a manager has to stay in the same position for three to six years to get promoted or transferred. Quite a large number of employees are frustrated by not being able to get promoted, though the salary and benefits are very good compared to most other companies, and the turnover rate is low. The percentage of managers leaving their present posts is no higher than 4 percent, and most of them do so only because they have reached retirement age.

Organization B is another leading manufacturer in Taiwan, whose profitability and corporate image are even better than organization A. Its mission statement and management philosophy are unclear. Similar to most organizations in the study, most of the managers are promoted from within. Different from organization A, the managers in organization B are promoted from an internal management path only, and not from engineering.

According to the human resources manager of firm B, the main difficulties they encounter are twofold. First, recruitment and placement of technicians and engineers is getting more difficult, due to the special nature of the industry and fluctuating market demand. Second, as a large organization, its organizational structure is getting rigid. As a result, few promotion opportunities can be offered to most employees for both management and engineering ladders; thus motivation is at risk.

The few managers not promoted from within were those who were transferred from the head office or another branch. The major criteria for promotion are outstanding performance and communication and management ability. Also, the small number of vacancies available is a critical factor.

Organization C is a multinational company. In addition to the head office located in Kaohsiung, Taiwan, it has branches operating in Malaysia and the United States. Thus, these managers have the opportunity to become expatriates.

A total of 1,100 people work for the company, and fifty among them are employed as managers. In this company, an engineer is likely to be promoted to a managing position after working for three to five years. Consistent with most surveys cited, the most important criteria for promotion are performance, managing ability, and communication skills. The turnover rate for managers in organization C is 2 to 3 percent.

The difficulty facing organization C is the common problem experienced by the average manufacturing company in Taiwan: labor shortages. Though great efforts are made, such as offering a variety of training and education programs and providing personal career planning consulting, the situation does not improve much.

Organization D is a public educational unit. In this organization, formal human resources planning has been done for years and is operating smoothly. However, being only one part of the whole educational system, most managers (department chiefs and chairs) are transferred from other units; only a few are recruited from civilian fields. Hence, the role of its human resources department is somewhat different from those in other organizations. In Organization D, the main function of the human resources department is making sure the policies set by top authorities are properly implemented, instead of making human resources plans of their own.

In addition to employees of these Taiwanese firms, a small sample of Taiwanese employees of four U.S. firms are included in this report. Briefly, they include one financial services organization, a durable and a nondurable manufacturing organization, and a petrochemical organization.

The organizations included in this study are all well-established firms, and human resources planning has long been a set policy. Each is offering a variety of career management activities either formally or informally, such as job posting, career counseling, performance review, career testing, job rotation, and skill training, among others.

In addition to formal career management programs, most organizations also use informal methods to influence employees to have the kinds of careers they desire for them. Taiwanese organizations are most likely to reward goal achievement, promote teamwork, offer appreciation, and declare the benefits of working for this particular organization when they shape employees' careers. In contrast, Taiwanese employed in U.S. firms thought their organizations were more likely to offer good pay and fringe benefits, use slogans, indirectly threaten them, or use family connections to influence their careers.

INDIVIDUAL CAREERS

Individual Characteristics

A total of 103 line managers in Taiwan participated in this study, and 20 of them were working for U.S. firms in Taiwan at the time of the interview. All of the respondents are Chinese; 90.2 percent are male and 90.2 percent are married. They have an average of 2.3 children and 4.3 dependents. The average age of the respondents is 40.9 years, and the oldest two are respondents in the service industry of U.S. firms in Taiwan.

Internal Career Beliefs

Career Goals. During the interviews, managers were asked to rate the importance of each of twenty-three career goals they may have on a 1 to 5 scale. The answers from the respondents in different organizations shown by nationality as well as by industry are included in Table 4.1.

It is interesting to compare these results with the results from the Jan (1992) study on entry-level Taiwanese college graduates. The Jan survey indicated that the major reasons to choose a particular firm, in order of importance, were personal interests, chance for promotion and development, job security, opportunity for learning, welfare benefits, and income. Regardless of firm nationality and industry, however, the present study in general depicts a somewhat different picture. The more important work goals appear to be meaningful work, personal growth, skills, contribution to organization, and family, friendship, and fun.

The samples from both studies highly valued interesting and meaningful work, knowledge, and skill development. However, the respondents of the earlier survey, all of whom were entry-level college graduates, also emphasized the importance of welfare benefits, job security, and income. On the other hand, the interviewees from the current study, mostly college graduates in their late thirties, cared more about friendship and contributions to their organizations and families. Job security, income, and fringe benefits were only secondary to them. This difference in work

Table 4.1
The Importance of Career Goals among Taiwanese Managers by Firm Nationality and Industry

	Taiwanese Firms				U.S. Firms	
	Manufacturing		Government			
Goals	Mean	S.D.	Mean	S.D.	Mean	S.D.
Income	3.6	.90	3.0[a]	.50	4.2[b]	.67
Prestige	3.7	.84	3.4	.90	3.8	.83
Power	3.0	.89	2.6[a]	.80	3.4[b]	.99
Skills	3.9	.90	4.0	.92	4.5[b]	.61
Creativity	3.5	.81	3.7	.95	4.2[b]	.52
Fun	4.2	.79	3.9	.78	3.7[b]	.88
Convenient hours	3.2	.88	3.1	.88	2.7	.98
Friendship	4.1	.74	4.0	.83	3.9	.93
Promotions	4.1	.84	3.5[a]	.91	4.1	.83
Variety	3.4	.89	3.1	.86	3.7[b]	.87
Autonomy	3.8	.74	3.4[a]	.93	4.0	.76
Achievement	3.9	.90	3.5[a]	.83	4.2[b]	.81
Residence	3.4	.79	3.4	1.06	3.3	.87
Contribution to organization	4.1	.81	4.0	.77	4.3	.64
Contribution to society	3.8	.85	3.8	.87	4.0	.73
Contribution to family	4.0	.84	3.6[a]	.75	4.1	.97
Security	3.9	.91	3.9	.80	3.6	1.05
Work conditions	3.6	.87	3.3	.82	3.7	.88
Keep busy	3.0	.81	3.1	1.01	2.8	1.03
Fringe benefits	3.5	.95	3.6	.87	3.6	1.21
Meaningful work	4.2	.75	4.0	.75	4.3	.64
Personal growth	4.3	.75	4.11	.81	4.6[b]	.61
Well being	3.6	.90	3.8	.78	4.0[b]	.73

Note: 1 = of little importance, 5 = extremely important.
a. Significant difference between Taiwanese manufacturing and government employees, $p < .05$.
b. Significant difference between all employees of Taiwanese firms and all employees of U.S. firms, $p < .05$.

goals makes it reasonable to contend that the career starters tend to be "economy people," whereas the relatively established are more inclined to be "social people" in terms of their values and goals.

If a career can be seen as a person's pattern of work life in a particular social context, in addition to understanding the mentality of how each person realizes and responds to his or her work experience, the relationship among the external social systems, the organizational structure, and individual beliefs can also be explored.

The concept of career management and planning is prevalent in Taiwan today. More than 90 percent of the Taiwanese managers taking part in this survey claimed to have carefully thought about their own careers before being interviewed and actually have made plans for developing their careers. Before Taiwan's rapid economic development, most people would take whatever jobs they could find. However, as riches accumulated, people began to think of developing a career where making money was not the sole high priority goal anymore. "They don't just look for jobs now; they choose jobs" (Shy, 1992). Many people even abandoned established careers to follow another career that they believed to better fit their values. It is widely believed that in Taiwan's open and mature society today one main reason for chasing dreams after forty is having achieved conventional financial success too early.

In the three Taiwanese manufacturing firms discussed, company policies were listed as the most significant career block. In fact, about one-fourth of the respondents considered firm policies to be a block to their career development. This may be primarily due to their frustration with the lack of promotion opportunities in these organizations. On the other hand, misperception between management and line managers may be another reason.

Human resources managers in each participating company confirmed that a variety of career management activities, such as job posting, career testing, and job rotation, have been used in these organizations. However, quite a large proportion of individual managers were not convinced, or not even aware, that there were company career management programs available to them.

The second most cited block was "myself." For example, quite a few respondents believed that their weak will and laziness could be the prime block to their careers. Organizational structure was another block most people considered. Again, this was due to the lack of promotion opportunities.

As to career helps, the immediate supervisor was considered to be a great help by most people. One manager said, "My supervisor has the most open leadership style, and he really cares about us. He encourages me to earn every training and growth opportunity. His encouragement has made me what I am today."

For respondents in manufacturing, personal skills and performance were also the factors many people believed to be helpful in developing the careers they desired. Characteristics of the job and "myself" both were also listed as primary helps.

In the public education unit, "myself" was listed as both the number-one block and help. Self-determination, hard work, perseverance, and patience were all considered to be helps from the individual. In contrast, lack of these traits formed the blocks to their careers. Organizational structure and company policies were also listed as primary blocks.

For employees in U.S. firms, immediate supervisors, spouses, friends, and co-workers were all helpful in attaining their desired career path. Among other helping factors, personal skills and performance were indicated as important.

Career Tactics. Gould and Penley (1984) named seven major categories of career tactics people could use in order to achieve their career goals. These career tactics are: (1) creating opportunities; (2) extended involvement; (3) enhancement; (4) opinion conformity; (5) self-nomination; (6) seeking guidance; and (7) networking. In general, education level is proportionate to extended involvement; and managers often adopt tactics other than enhancement and opinion conformity.

The findings of the present survey largely conformed to these conclusions. According to the average scores listed in Table 4.2, the career strategies Taiwanese managers employed in both Taiwanese firms and U.S. firms were most likely to use were working hard, doing their job well, learning more about the business, getting more education, and gaining rapport with their subordinates. Most Taiwanese managers employed in Taiwanese firms would also do what their boss wanted, while doing better than their peers is highest ranked for Taiwanese managers employed in U.S. firms. Threatening to leave, getting help from God, and getting a second job were least commonly used strategies for both groups. On the other hand, Taiwanese firm managers were much more reluctant to leave it to fate than U.S. firm managers, while the U.S. group was more reluctant to get career guidance than the former.

Career Outcomes

Though the definition of "success" varies among people, respect and recognition from others, having a sense of achievement, and being able to fulfill challenges were the most frequent answers to the question, How would you define career success for yourself? In the present study, 90 percent of the respondents could be classified as interpreting career success intrinsically. The answers of two managers in organization D are most representative of this inclination. One said, "Career success means the greatest contribution I can make in my current work." Another said, "Career success is having confidence in work."

To compare subjective career success between Taiwanese managers and those of other nations, Peng and Shyi (1994) adopted identical coding procedures to investigate respondents from Hong Kong (*n* = 71), Japan (*n* = 30), Singapore (*n* = 29), and Thailand (*n* = 24). They found that while a majority of the interviewees showed an intrinsic orientation toward career success, the percentages varied from 65 percent (Singapore) to 50 percent

Table 4.2
Career Tactics Used by Taiwanese Managers

Career Tactics	Taiwanese Firms		U.S. Firms		
	Mean	S.D.	Mean	S.D.	P Value
Work hard	4.0	.80	4.3	.79	
Work long hours	3.4	.98	3.2	1.19	
Do job well	4.3	.81	4.7	.49	*
Do something noticeable	3.3	.79	3.5	.95	
Do what boss wants	4.0	.86	3.8	1.00	
Act humble	3.2	.92	2.9	1.20	
Assertively ask	2.8	.84	2.8	1.30	
Exchange favors	3.2	.83	2.7	1.30	
Threaten to leave	1.5	.61	1.4	.68	
Ask powerful to help	2.3	.92	2.4	1.10	
Develop an action plan	3.1	.87	3.7	1.10	
Seek help from friends	3.1	.80	3.3	1.30	
Show loyalty to organization	3.6	.91	4.0	.97	
Show loyalty to boss	3.2	1.10	3.7	1.00	
Learn more about business	4.1	.72	4.7	.45	***
Get more education	4.2	.79	4.8	.44	***
Rapport with subordinates	4.2	.76	4.5	.61	*
Do better than peers	3.9	.71	4.8	.42	***
Become indispensable	3.8	.81	3.4	1.20	
Get important information	2.9	.97	3.6	1.15	*
Conform to expectations	3.4	.81	3.9	1.00	*
Get help from family	2.7	1.02	2.3	1.40	
Get help from God	1.7	.77	1.6	.83	
Change family to fit job	2.5	.81	2.4	.96	
Get a transfer	2.8	.67	3.1	1.00	
Get a job in new organization	2.7	.73	3.2	1.50	
Get a second job	2.2	.81	1.8	1.30	
Create a job in organization	2.6	.89	2.8	1.30	
Get more control of job	3.7	.65	3.3	1.11	
Change way of thinking	3.0	.71	3.0	1.50	
Network	3.4	.81	3.8	.77	*
Start own company	2.6	1.00	2.4	1.60	
Let self be recognized	3.2	.77	2.2	1.10	**
Leave it to fate	2.0	.84	3.6	1.12	***
Tell boss own career plan	2.9	2.89	3.2	1.22	
Get career guidance	3.1	.85	1.0	1.50	***

Note: 1 = very unlikely, 5 = very likely.
*Significantly different, $p < .05$.
**$p < .01$.
***$p < .001$.

(Japan). If Taiwanese managers indeed value more strongly intrinsic values of career success than their counterparts in the neighboring countries, organizations could be sensitive enough to provide more psychological rewards to meet their needs if they wish to motivate their employees.

A survey on the value of success was conducted by a leading magazine, *Commonwealth Monthly* (Jiang, 1994). Among the 1,282 subjects, the answers to the question, What is success?, include the following: a happy family (60.5%); being able to do what I like to do (36.5%); career success (36.2%); health (43.6%); personal wealth (10.1%); self-growth, use of skills (26.1%); high social status and reputation (3.0%); and contribution to society and others (18.3%). As can be seen, personal wealth is generally considered to be low in importance, and is not an important indicator of success in either the present study or the 1994 study.

Despite efforts to attain desired career goals, people may not always get what they expect. When the respondents were asked about the chance of achieving career success in their organizations, more than 60 percent of respondents were positive about achieving career success by doing what they do now. When asked further about how they would react if they failed to achieve the goals they desired, most people revealed the philosophy of "whatever will be, will be." One answered the following way: "Whether to make an effort is under my command, but whether it will succeed is the decision of Heaven." Another interviewee said, "In that case, it means that I have no control over it. Then, I will still do my job well and try to take it lightly." Some people took a more positive attitude: "I will not give up. I can wait for opportunities."

Satisfaction. In a survey by *Commonwealth Magazine* (1994), about 70 percent of the respondents were satisfied with family life, and more than 50 percent were satisfied with personal health and being able to do things they liked to do. However, "career success" was one of the items that showed a lower degree of satisfaction. Fewer than 40 percent of interviewees believed they currently had achieved their expected goals.

In the present study, the mean scores for the questions, In general, how satisfied are you with meeting your career goals so far in your life?, and In general, how satisfied are you with your life?, were 3.05 and 3.40, respectively, showing a moderate satisfaction with careers and life in general. On the other hand, about 60 percent of the respondents said their career development had met their expectations.

Table 4.3 exhibits the satisfaction level the respondents felt about the various aspects of their jobs in their present organizations. In general, the satisfaction levels of each item were close; no single items were extraordinarily above or below average.

Table 4.3 also shows that most people were moderately satisfied with what they gained from work. However, employees had a strong commitment toward their organizations. More than 95 percent of managers of Tai-

Table 4.3
Career Satisfaction by Industry

Satisfaction with	Manufacturing		Government		
	Mean	S.D.	Mean	S.D.	P Value
Income	3.3	.60	3.6	.61	**
Prestige	3.1	.77	3.7	.59	***
Power	3.1	.85	3.4	.61	
Skills	3.2	.78	3.4	.84	
Creativity	3.1	.79	3.2	.66	
Fun	3.1	.81	3.6	.56	**
Convenient hours	3.4	.73	3.6	.80	
Friendship	3.5	.69	3.7	.63	
Promotions	2.9	.86	3.1	.98	
Variety	3.1	.73	3.3	.64	
Autonomy	3.4	.69	3.4	.76	
Achievement	3.3	.90	3.3	.75	
Residence	3.6	.91	3.6	.91	
Contribution to organization	3.7	.86	3.7	.57	
Contribution to society	3.3	.87	3.5	.72	
Contribution to family	3.5	.82	3.3	.86	
Security	3.5	.90	3.5	.95	
Work conditions	3.3	.84	3.5	.72	
Keep busy	3.4	.75	3.6	.56	
Fringe benefits	3.2	.71	3.2	.78	
Meaningful work	3.4	1.00	3.5	.67	
Personal growth	3.5	.97	3.5	.72	
Well being	3.2	.83	3.3	.74	

Note: 1 = very dissatisfied, 5 = very satisfied.
*Significantly different, $p < .05$.
**$p < .01$.
***$p < .001$.

wanese organizations and 100 percent of Taiwanese managers of U.S. organizations agreed with the statement, "This organization means a lot to me."

CONCLUSIONS

This chapter provides a general picture of what career management programs and individual career plans are like in Taiwan. Some weaknesses of the study should be pointed out. As the sample size is small and the professions of the subjects are relatively limited, the subjects of the study are more or less similar in background; for instance, the majority of them were engineers in manufacturing industries. As is usually the case, a person's views are influenced by his or her background and experiences; thus, respondents revealed a high degree of conformity in many questions. If different types of industries had been chosen, greater differences among organizations might have appeared.

Using only large organizations was another limitation of this study. Most people enter large-scale organizations for similar reasons, such as job security, reasonable benefits, welfare, and salaries, so the findings may not be that representative of Taiwanese employees of smaller organizations.

In spite of these limitations, in recent years career management has captured much attention in this Chinese society. This has occurred despite the fact that some smaller companies have not established concrete measures dealing with the issues.

Implications for the Individual

As a Chinese proverb goes, "Heaven helps those who help themselves," and it seems that most Chinese people are convinced of this truth. As indicated from this study, although they say they do not believe in relying on fate as a career tactic, most individuals do accept their destiny as fate. If they want more advancement in their careers, they may have to take more proactive strategies to achieve their desired career goals. Those strategies that proved useful and helpful include learning more about the business, getting more education, working hard, acquiring more training, and continuing development.

Implications for Organizations

Likewise, Taiwanese firms can benefit from implementing more extensive career management programs. In several instances, firms could benefit from linking the desire for further education with important organizational goals, because education is a highly valued career tactic. Among the most common activities provided by organizations are skill training, job rotation, mentoring, performance review, career information, and job posting.

At the individual level, the career goals that the Chinese managers valued most were personal growth, meaningful work, making contributions, promotion, and friendship. Extrinsic rewards such as income and fringe benefits do not seem to be so important as those listed previously. The career tactics used most often include working hard, doing a job well, getting more education, doing better than peers, and developing rapport with subordinates. Frequently, adopting these tactics to advance one's career is consistent with the belief that diligence, education, and harmony are among the qualities emphasized in the Confucian culture. Organizations that provide opportunities for employees to satisfy these career goals could benefit in many ways.

REFERENCES

Central Daily. (1994, September 14). A thirty-thousand increase in medium and small enterprises than last year.

China Daily. (1996, July 14). Taiwan was the sixth biggest trade partner of mainland China.

Council of Labor Affairs, Executive Yuan. (1992). *Report on the enterprises' employment and management system and labor's perception of work in Taiwan area.* Taipei, Republic of China: the Council.

Council of Labor Affairs, Executive Yuan. (1993). *Study on the participation rate of women in Taiwan.* Taipei, Republic of China: the Council.

Council of Labor Affairs, Executive Yuan. (1993). *Work experience survey.* Taipei, Republic of China: the Council.

Council of Labor Affairs, Executive Yuan. (June, 1996). *Monthly bulletin of labor Statistics, Taiwan area.* Taipei, Republic of China: the Council.

Council for Economic Development and Planning, Executive Yuan. (1991). *Human Resources management report.* Taipei, Republic of China: the Council.

Council for Economic Development and Planning, Executive Yuan. (1992). *Human Resources management report.* Taipei, Republic of China: the Council.

Council for Economic Development and Planning, Executive Yuan. (1993). *Human Resources management report.* Taipei, Republic of China: the Council.

Directorate-General of Budgets, Accounting & Statistics, Executive Yuan. (1992). *National wealth survey.* Taipei, Republic of China: the Directorate General.

Directorate-General of Budgets, Accounting & Statistics, Executive Yuan. (1993). *Survey of the distribution of household income.* Taipei, Republic of China: the Directorate General.

Directorate-General of Budgets, Accounting & Statistics, Executive Yuan. (1996). *Monthly statistics of the Republic of China.* Taipei, Republic of China: the Directorate General.

Directorate of Statistics, Executive Yuan. (1993). *Comparison of monthly salaries of professions: January to July.* Taipei, Republic of China: the Directorate General.

Gen, Y. G. (1992). CEOs who refuse to go job hopping: A survey on the career planning of CEOs in Taiwan. *Leader Monthly, 79,* 14–16.

Gould, S., & Penley, L. E. (1984). Career strategies and salary progression: A study of their relationships in a municipal bureaucracy. *Organizational Behavior and Human Performance, 34,* 244–265.

Hwang, K. K. (1983). Organization patterns and employees' morale in Taiwan. *Journal of Graduate School of Ethnology, 56,* 145–193.

International Monetary Foundation. (1994). *International financial statistics.* New York: United Nations.

Jan, T. S. (1992). Survey on the work preferences of entry-level college graduates. *Management Monthly, 215,* 112–118.

Jiang, S. I. (1994, February). Are Taiwanese happy? *Commonwealth Monthly,* 50–55.

Liao, C. L. (1992). The latest condition of enterprises' requirements and recruitment of employees. *Management Monthly, 215*, 94–110.

Liu, G. L. (1994). The coming of the era where service industry outweighs manufacturing. *Excellence Monthly, 118*, 166–170.

Ministry of Economic Affairs. (1994). *Briefing on the foreign investment of Taiwanese enterprises.* Taipei, Republic of China: the Ministry.

Ministry of Economic Affairs, Statistics Department. (1994). *Economic situation report.* Taipei, Republic of China: the Ministry.

Ministry of Interior. (1993). *Population statistics in Taiwan area.* Taipei, Republic of China: the Ministry.

Ministry of Transportation & Communications. (1991). *Tourism bureau: A glance at Taiwan.* Taipei, Republic of China: the Ministry.

Nixon, R. (1994). *Beyond peace.* New York: Random House.

Peng, T. K., &, Shyi, Y. P. (1994). *Perceived career success and intrinsic/extrinsic careerists: A study of managers from Pacific Rim countries.* Proceedings of the 2nd Biennial International Conference on Advances in Management, Calgary, Canada.

Shapiro, D. (May 10, 1993). A siren across the straits. *Time*, 32–33.

Sheen, W. T. (1993). Five big families taking over Taiwan. *Excellence Monthly, 109*, 28-33.

Shih, R. (1991). *Career planning system in manufacturing enterprises.* Thesis of Graduate School of Business Management. National Chung Hsing University, Republic of China.

Shinn Yih Cultural Foundation. (1993). *Report on work values of employees in Taiwan area.* Taipei, Republic of China: the Foundation.

Shy, G. W. (1992). Choosing the job rather than looking for the job. *Career Magazine, 79.*

CHAPTER FIVE

Careers of Japanese Managers

Masao Baba
Cherlyn Skromme Granrose
Allan Bird

Since 1989 and the bursting of the Japanese economic bubble, observers of Japan have suggested that the Japanese management system is on the verge of a fundamental shift—a shift that will materially affect the livelihood and careers of most Japanese workers. Four factors have been identified as contributing to this significant change (Beck & Beck, 1994). First, the Japanese workforce is aging at a rapid rate, causing substantial pressure on the internal labor market systems of most firms. Second, the maturing of numerous industries has led to slower growth in the economy, making it difficult for firms to maintain career employment practices. Third, diversification attempts by firms to move out of slower growth industries have been accompanied by an increasing willingness to accept mid-career hires. Finally, the internationalization of Japanese firms and the Japanese economy has intensified competition and broken down resistance to new ways of managing workers. These pressures have continued into the late 1990s (Watanabe & Holley, 1996).

It is in this context that we undertook an examination of careers in Japanese organizations. Our intent was to assess the current state of affairs, and in the process develop a more complete picture of Japanese perceptions of careers and career-related issues. What follows is an overview of the social, cultural, political, economic, and organizational context in which Japanese careers unfold. This is followed by an examination of career practices in specific Japanese firms and U.S. firms doing business in Japan. These data were collected between 1992 and 1994, just as the economy of Japan began to adjust to a major restructuring. While the background material focuses on Japan's recent past, the new data begin to address career issues important to the future.

NATIONAL CHARACTERISTICS INFLUENCING CAREER OPTIONS

Identity: Resources and History

Most of the 126 million people who live in the seventh most populous country in the world are concentrated in the valleys and the coastal flatlands. Japan is one of the few Asian nations that shows both low fertility and low mortality rates (Ogawa, Jones, & Williamson, 1993; Keizai Koho Center, 1995). The 1994 life expectancy at birth was seventy-seven years for men and eighty-three years for women. With the world's most rapidly aging population, the prospective rise in the proportion of elderly people after the turn of the century has long-term economic and social significance for careers of Japanese managers.

World War II devastated much of Japan's economic foundation; however, in the postwar decades economic expansion was extremely rapid. Until 1973, the economy grew at an average of 10 percent annually, a rate unprecedented in the records of major nations.

In the past two decades, Japan has developed greater economic interdependence with other countries of South East Asia. Yen appreciation and high labor costs have encouraged many manufacturing firms to relocate plants from Japan to Malaysia, Indonesia, Thailand, and other developing countries in Asia (United Nations, 1993; Ozawa, 1995; Watanabe & Holley, 1996; Wood, 1994). The recent slowdown in economic growth may lead to alternative economic policies in the future (Wood, 1994). The major issues facing Japan in the future include coping with a large, aging labor force and an increasingly elderly population in an economy which is experiencing a rapid decline in growth rate. This change in economic circumstances provides a major challenge to future economic planning.

National Policies Affecting Careers

Economic Planning and Policies.   During the Meiji period of Japanese history (1868–1912), a modern national government system including cabinet, legislative, and judicial systems began an economic policy promoting modern industries under direct government management. The government also supported a public school system to provide an educated labor force.

The National Labor Standards Act (1941) set a six-day, forty-eight-hour work week that was shortened to forty hours in 1988. Immigration control laws restrict imported labor, and import policies carefully define permitted and forbidden import products. These formal legal restrictions, many imposed by U.S. postwar administrators, persist and are supplemented by many more informal customs of Japanese origin (Aoto, Fukuzawa, Hoyoshi, & Yage, 1988).

Educational Laws and Policies. Japan's rigorous system of education includes six years of elementary school, three years of middle school, three years of high school, and four years of college. Everyone must attend school for five and a half days per week (240 days/year) for at least nine years. Although high school is voluntary, more than 95 percent of Japanese youngsters now complete this course. More than 45 percent of upper secondary school graduates enter institutions of higher learning.

One measure of the efficacy of the Japanese educational system is the performance of ten- and fourteen-year-olds on standardized tests given to the children of nineteen industrialized nations. Japanese students scored the highest in most subjects. Also, the current literacy rate is 99 percent—one of the highest in the world (Japanese Ministry of Education, 1994).

Competition to attend prestigious high schools and universities is very high because graduation from esteemed schools increases the opportunity for employment in a prominent firm. Entrance examinations screen applicants for private junior high, high school, and university education, and results determine access to both the institution and the field of study (Tung, 1984). Graduation in March coincides with large business hiring cycles; about 95 percent of male and 97 percent of female college graduates enter white collar ranks, and about 54 percent of male and 16 percent of female high school graduates enter blue collar positions on April 1, the beginning of the Japanese fiscal year. However since the burst of the bubble economy, Japanese graduates have experienced a hard time finding the jobs they wished to get, largely because of business restructuring policies. This is reflected in the recent rise in the unemployment rate (Japanese Ministry of Labor, 1995).

Nationally Shared Career Beliefs and Norms

Work Values and the Meaning of Work. In national surveys, diligence and discipline were identified as dominant characteristics of Japanese people (Tung, 1984). Cross-national comparisons of work values highlight specific Japanese work values. Hofstede studied work values of 50,000 workers in forty-four different countries (1981). He found significant differences across cultures with regard to four values that influence how people approach their work: power distance, uncertainty avoidance, individualism, and masculinity.

Compared to other countries, Japan exhibits a moderate to high power distance. That is, many believe that there should be clear distinctions between superiors and subordinates, but also that subordinates should participate to some degree in decision-making activities.

The source of this orientation to power distance may be rooted in a Japanese version of Confucianism which is embodied in a seventh-century code of conduct—Prince Shotoku's Seventeen Article Constitution. Subjects are exhorted to submit to rulers and rulers are admonished to nurture subjects in relationships of mutual support (Reischauer & Craig, 1978).

Hofstede's second value, uncertainty avoidance, refers to the extent to which a culture has a tolerance for uncertainty, particularly about the future. Japan scores quite high on this dimension. To avoid uncertainty in employment situations and labor relations, Japanese companies seek to maintain internal labor markets with few ports of entry and exits. This is buttressed by institutional practices favoring membership in known industrial groups and the development of strong affiliate connections and spin-offs whereby retiring and redundant employees can be seconded or permanently transferred to other members of the group. A low tolerance for uncertainty is also reflected in intensive selection processes that are designed to develop a comprehensive picture of the potential hire. Postrecruitment socialization continues the process by assimilating and acculturating new employees into a strong corporate culture. This reduces the uncertainty associated with admitting newcomers by developing a single set of shared organizational values.

Japan is a low individualism culture, meaning that its members value affiliation and belonging to a group (collectivism). For most members of the labor force in Japan, the most important collectivity they belong to is the company (Triandis, Bontempo, Villareal, Asai, & Lucca, 1988). Practices such as lifetime employment, no-layoff policies, and the paternalistic treatment of employees by the company in the form of company-sponsored benefits are a reflection of collectivist values.

According to Hofstede (1981), Japan ranks as a highly masculine country, due to the strong distinctions made between male and female gender role norms within the society, as well as the emphasis on achievement and the acquisition of material wealth. The positive evaluation of masculinity also influences norms for who should hold particular work roles in Japanese society.

Norms Regarding Labor Force Participation. Western conceptions of Japanese employees are founded almost entirely on a view of male white collar employees. The concepts of lifetime employment, a seniority-based wage system, and job rotation apply most appropriately to this one class of Japanese employees. In Japan this type of worker is known as the "salaryman."

Although women play a vital role in business, because of strict social norms reinforced by company policies, they are not represented in top managerial positions in large Japanese firms. Women constitute 40.5 percent of the labor force, but about 30 percent of them are in part-time positions. Women made up 6.4 percent of all *Kakaricho* (section head), 2.6 percent of all *Kacho* (department head), and 1.4 percent of *Bucho* (division head) in 1994 (Japanese Ministry of Labor, 1995).

There have been some recent developments in white collar career opportunities for female employees with the passage of the Equal Employment Opportunity Act in 1986. Companies such as Seibu (the large department store) have sought to develop managerial tracks that parallel but do not overlap male white collar tracks. Although a handful of women are middle and senior managers in large firms, women are more frequently found in managerial roles in non-Japanese firms or in small- to medium-size domestic firms in Japan. This is due to the societal norm excluding women from the workplace as well as to the strictures of major corporations that do not extend benefits to this "risky" class of employees. Because Japanese firms retain employees for an extended period of time in order to offset the high costs of socialization and training, large firms believe (and many Japanese women themselves tend to agree) that the investment may not be worthwhile. Since many women retire when they become pregnant, in order to devote themselves to enhancing their children's educational fortunes in the competitive race to the best universities, firms have tended to exclude women from this process.

National Career Behavior Patterns

Distribution of the Japanese Labor Force. The current size of the labor force is approximately 64.5 million people. Six percent are agricultural and farm workers. The second largest group (34%) are involved in the secondary or manufacturing sector. The remaining 60 percent are service workers.

For the past five, years the unemployment rate has been fluctuating from 2.1 percent to 2 percent. It is important to note, however, that Japan defines unemployment in a unique way. First, about 32.5 percent of female workers are not full-time and are not reported as unemployed. Additionally, the number of hours that one must work in order to be considered employed is substantially lower than twenty hours a week. If the unemployment rate is broken down by age group, the lowest unemployment is found in the 45–54 category. The 25–44 and 55–59 age groups are slightly higher and comparable in unemployment rate. Recent efforts to pressure higher paid senior managers to take early retirement may change this picture in the future (Watanabe & Holley, 1996).

Employment is about equally divided between those working for large firms and those working for small- and medium-sized firms. Because larger firms are part of a network of related companies tied to smaller suppliers of raw materials and parts, large and small firms may be interconnected and employees may move from larger parent companies to smaller subsidiaries and suppliers. Some scholars argue that it is employment in the smaller firms linked to larger firms that is key to Japan's economic success (Friedman, 1988). With larger firms shifting some business to less expensive suppliers in South East Asia, rather than smaller Japanese firms, the extent to which current economic changes reinforce or sever these ties may contribute to the future shape of career opportunities for Japanese employees.

ORGANIZATIONAL CHARACTERISTICS INFLUENCING CAREER OPTIONS

Organizational Career Processes

To understand the post World War II Japanese labor market, it is better to think in terms of employees and firms rather than jobs and skills. Unlike Western labor markets where companies recruit people to fill specific jobs requiring special skills, in Japan employees are hired for their latent potential, with the expectation that they can be trained to work in any number of jobs. At the completion of entry training, new employees are assigned to their first positions, where they may spend anywhere from one to three years learning the ropes of the organization and establishing their relationship networks among peers and superiors. From this point until retirement, the standard will be to rotate jobs every three to five years. Promotions tend to come slowly at first, with the initial promotion coming as early as year four or as late as year eight. Education, training, and skill development are continuous, instigated by the firm and employees (Abegglen & Stalk, 1985).

Job rotation during this time moves in one of two directions. "Fast-trackers," who have been tabbed as the managerial elite, will rotate through different divisions or areas of the company. Those less likely to advance to senior managerial positions are more likely to find that job rotations move them across functional disciplines as well as divisional boundaries, but fast-trackers generally remain within a particular functional discipline, such as marketing.

Most firms pursue an early forced retirement system whereby less productive employees are encouraged to relocate to affiliated firms for lower pay and benefits. Even for productive workers, the standard retirement age is normally between fifty-five and sixty years old, with fifty-eight being the current average. This mandatory retirement age is becoming a serious problem as life expectancy grows. Firms are reluctant to change this policy, however, as economic slowdowns stimulate smaller labor force requirements (Adams, Peterson, & Schwind, 1987).

The tighter the economic times, the more difficult promotion becomes, the more bonuses are tied to performance rather than seniority, and the more younger managers leapfrog over older managers into responsible positions. In spite of pressure to tighten their economic belts, early predictions that Japanese firms would be forced to give up traditional security-providing human resources practices seem exaggerated and long-term employment remains a staple of the male managerial ranks (Adams, Peterson, & Schwind, 1987; Pucik, 1984; Watanabe & Holley, 1996).

Organizational Career Behavior

One of the best known longitudinal career studies of Japanese managers employed in large firms was conducted by Mitsuru Wakabayashi of Nagoya University and George Graen of the University of Cincinnati (1984; 1988). Beginning in 1972, this study followed seventy-one managers of one cohort entering a large department store from hiring to middle management. Superior–supervisor relationships, first job characteristics, selection test results, intermediate job performance, and immediate supervisor ranking were used to predict year 7 promotion rates, salary, and bonuses. University ranking was not significant, but all other predictors contributed to promotion and pay variability (Wakabayashi & Graen, 1984). Later reports of a thirteen-year follow-up confirmed earlier findings in most respects (Wakabayashi, Graen, Graen, & Graen, 1988) but focused on the effects of early experience and of later job challenge after the first round of socialization transfers and initial promotions. Promotion and bonus after thirteen years were most strongly predicted by early performance appraisal results and supervisor interactions, with entry potential becoming less important.

This description of managerial career patterns in one firm is consistent with reports of typical Japanese careers in other large firms in the 1970s and 1980s (Ouchi & Johnson, 1978; Abegglen & Stalk, 1985). The study presented in this chapter seeks to describe in greater detail the organizational system and the individual managerial characteristics of Japanese managers employed in three large Japanese firms in the 1990s and to compare these to Japanese managers employed by two U.S. firms currently operating in Japan.

THE ORGANIZATIONS

Organizational Identity

The Japanese data were gathered from five organizations; three were Japanese and two were U.S. The first Japanese firm (K) is a large manufacturing firm established in 1917 and employing approximately 15,081 people in 1991. It has offices in North America, South America, Asia, Europe, and Africa. Its current mission statement emphasizes "Growth, Groupwide, and Global" integration.

The second Japanese firm, K W, is a bank established in 1920. It currently has seventeen branch offices in Japan and employed 482 people in 1993.

The third Japanese firm, M, is in the real estate business. This firm was established in 1969 and had 1,480 employees in 1991. It has holdings in Japan, the United States, Hong Kong, Australia, Spain, Amsterdam, and Bangkok.

The two U.S. firms doing business in Japan were quite different. Firm C is a large American insurance company that entered the Japanese market by formulating a joint venture with several Japanese insurance firms, eventually buying them out. There were actually four separate entities: reinsurance, life insurance, investments, and general insurance. Each had different human resources departments and separate staffing policies. Managers reported that it was difficult, if not impossible, to transfer from one part of this firm to another because of strong organizational boundaries. Yet the central offices of these firms were located in the same building in Tokyo and all had the parent company name and logo as part of the artifacts of corporate culture. All four entities are represented in the sample reported here.

The second U.S. firm is a global petrochemical company that did not take over a Japanese firm. Instead, it hired Japanese managers, individually, to develop a Tokyo office.

Organizational Career Norms

Organizational human resources policies were obtained from firm documents and from interviews with vice presidents of human resources. Both U.S. firms had large Pacific regional offices in Hong Kong, and these offices represented the home companies in most policy issues.

The Japanese firms have used a traditional core of male employees hired into clerk positions from specific universities then slowly promoted into managerial positions. Employees typically spent four to six years in clerical positions before receiving first promotions to *Kakaricho*. After another four to six years, which might include lateral transfers, they might be promoted again, a few eventually attaining *Kacho* or even *Bucho* status. Generous training programs and fringe benefits including housing, meals, transportation, medical care, and recreational facilities were complemented with twice-yearly bonuses. This is comparable to other reports of Japanese human resources systems published in the 1980s (Ouchi, 1981; Pucik, 1984; Yeh & Phatak, 1987).

The U.S. petrochemical company followed common U.S. human resources practices, but the U.S. insurance firm had a hybrid system with older employees experiencing and expecting traditional Japanese policies of high job security and generous fringe benefits and younger employees and the home office expecting the firm to provide higher salaries, more rapid promotions, and leaner fringe benefits. The human resources managers in the U.S.-based insurance firms were in an extremely difficult position, trapped between many employees' Japanese expectations and the home office's U.S. policies.

Organizational Career Processes

When human resources managers and line managers were asked about organizational career policies, some similarities and a few striking differences appeared between the U.S.-based and Japanese-based firms. In the Japanese subsidiaries of U.S. firms, positions were equally likely to be filled by hiring, promotion, or transfer, whereas 73 percent of Japanese managers in Japanese firms reported that job transfer was the most common way to fill a position. Thirty percent of Japanese managers in Japanese firms and only 10 percent of Japanese managers in U.S. firms reported that their company had formal career paths that most employees followed.

Similar to findings in the Wakabayashi and Graen study (1988), the criteria for transfer and for promotion were divided among job skills, organizational needs, and work attitudes, with Japanese firms slightly more likely to use firm needs and workers' attitudes and U.S. firms slightly more likely to use job skills as criteria for changing employees' jobs. All Japanese reported that either upper management or upper management and their immediate supervisors were likely to make promotion decisions, but the senior human resources manager in each site also had significant power to influence the career paths of managers.

Specific career management techniques in Japanese organizations relied heavily on skill training (81%) and testing (67%), providing general information about the organization (63%), and job rotation (53%). Formal performance reviews were reported by 39 percent of Japanese managers employed in Japanese firms and 86 percent of Japanese managers in Japanese offices of U.S. firms, but many managers did not know the actual outcome of their reviews. U.S. firms were also more likely to use coaching (54%) and counseling (24%) for employee career management.

In addition to formal career programs, organizations often had multiple methods for convincing employees to follow career paths beneficial to the firm. Japanese managers in Japanese firms report that the general culture of the firm (which offered appreciation for doing whatever was best for the organization) was the strongest influence on their careers (see Table 5.1). Japanese managers employed in U.S. firms reported most commonly that the firm set specific performance goals and offered good pay and fringe benefits to influence their careers.

In summary, the large organizations participating in this study reflect a range of career options available to Japanese managers. Most managers remain in traditional Japanese firms, adhering to career paths directed by

Table 5.1
Organizational Influence Tactics Reported by Employees

Tactics	U.S. Firms in Japan (n=30)	Japanese Firms (n=60)
Songs	1.97	2.98*
Pay	3.30	3.20
Fringe benefits	3.30	3.20
Working conditions	3.14	3.24
Employee influence	3.43	2.98*
Threats	2.07	2.45
Teamwork	2.97	3.30
Rational arguments	2.30	2.77*
Nationalism	1.70	2.31*
Appreciation	3.07	3.71*
Family connections	1.86	2.53*
Firm pride	2.70	3.25*
Information sharing	3.37	3.45
Career opportunities	3.0	2.97
Career training	3.10	3.17
Management culture	3.0	3.74*
Family-like culture	3.07	2.70
Performance goals	3.43	3.23

Note: 1 = very unlikely to use, 5 = very likely to use.
*Japanese and U.S. firms are significantly different, $p \leq .05$.

strong norms of corporate loyalty in exchange for security and appreciation. A smaller number belong to U.S. and other foreign firms with career policies traditional to other cultures, such as U.S. firms directing careers through performance goals and pay. Another small minority work in firms that try to blend policies appropriate to the Japanese culture with policies used in distant home offices. The impact of employment in each of these settings is seen in the career patterns of individual line managers.

THE INDIVIDUALS

We asked all line managers to describe themselves and their family context, then to relate their career history, and finally to respond to qualitative and quantitative questions about their career beliefs and attitudes. By combining each of these kinds of information, we offer a complex picture of the careers of one sample of Japanese managers.

The sample was selected in consultation with the vice presidents of human resources to represent all departments, levels, and performance abilities present in the firms at each location. To participate, managers had to have at least one year of work experience (six months with the current firm) and either supervise others or have a comparable management-level technical position.

For the Japanese firms, questionnaires were translated into Japanese by the senior Japanese author and three of his associates. Japanese managers employed in U.S. firms were given one week to complete the English questionnaires. After completing the questionnaires, they participated in an interview (thirty minutes to two hours long) to clarify questions, enrich open-ended responses, and confirm completion of all items. Managers also were given the option of having a translator present. Four managers in one office of the U.S. insurance firm used this option, even though the U.S. home office had assured the researcher that all Japanese managers of this firm had to use English in their daily work and were fluent English speakers. The primary interviewers, representing U.S. or Japanese universities, were clearly separate from the organization, and all interview data except the four interviews with the translator present maintained complete confidentiality and independence from the organization.

Individual Identity of Line Managers

A total of ninety-six Japanese line managers were interviewed for this study—sixty-six men employed in Japanese firms and twenty-five men and five women employed in Japanese subsidiaries of U.S. firms. Seventy-nine percent of those employed in U.S. firms and 92 percent of those employed in Japanese firms were married, 41 percent to spouses who also were employed. Many of the employed wives (more than 40%) held full-time clerical positions.

The age of these managers ranged from twenty-five to sixty-four years old, with an average of forty-three years old. Children were evenly distributed in age from newborns to young adulthood, with most families having one or two children. Almost all respondents said they were Buddhist, with a smaller minority (14%) reporting no religious affiliation. Only seven did not have a college education, and slightly more than half had a graduate degree. Their field of study as undergraduates was evenly distributed among business, science, engineering, and the social sciences.

The relatively high educational status of these managers was an extension of their family histories. Most had fathers who were entrepreneurs (24%), managers (18%), or professionals (14%), with the remainder coming from families of clerical, service, or agricultural workers. Half had mothers who were employed at one time.

Because we asked firms to help select a sample that represented all levels, performance abilities, and departments, we had little control over the selection process. The sample is probably skewed toward better performers and higher levels, with approximately half holding positions one to four levels from the top and the rest holding positions four to ten levels from the top of their organizations. A preponderance of older workers is typical of many Japanese firms, however. The pathways these managers took to gain these positions constitute their external careers.

External Career Patterns

Descriptions of career patterns were obtained first by asking participants to describe their first jobs after leaving school and any occupational changes they had made subsequently. Almost none had changed their actual occupation, but most had changed jobs four to five times in their careers.

A specific job history yielded information on every job held for six or more months in which the person worked twenty or more hours per week. These Japanese managers reported working forty-five to fifty hours per week from three to forty-one years. Most employees of Japanese firms had worked for only one firm and had received one to five promotions and about as many lateral moves. Japanese employees of U.S. Japanese subsidiaries had worked for two or three firms and had similar promotion patterns but fewer lateral transfers. Japanese managers working for Japanese firms had almost double the organizational tenure (x_J = 20.80 years, $x_{U.S.}$ = 12.25 years) and had spent over twice as long in their current job (x_J = 4.58 years, $x_{U.S.}$ = 1.89 years).

When asked how long they expected to stay with their present firms, most reported a number equivalent to the number of years until their retirement. Japanese managers who worked for Japanese firms were noticeably reluctant to answer this particular question ($N_{missing\ values}$ = 29) or responded with a general statement such as "as long as my company wants me" or "until the firm tells me to go." All managers reported that it was about equally likely or unlikely that they could get an equal or better position in their current firm, but Japanese managers of Japanese firms believed it was much less likely they could get such a position in another firm (x_J = 2.16, $x_{U.S.}$ = 2.87, $p \geq .05$).

A more vivid picture of external career patterns is apparent in individual career descriptions. One Japanese manager working for a Japanese firm reported this career history:

When I got out of school I joined this company because my father had worked for the company and, also, some of my friends. I began as a clerk in the sales division. After a few years I was transferred to the production division. I was promoted, and eventually I was sent overseas as a branch manager. When I returned, I went back to the production division as a manager.

A manager employed by the Japanese subsidiary of the U.S. insurance firm gave this as his career history:

I joined a large Japanese firm first because it provided good possibilities and was worth doing. I worked for them for sixteen years, first as a clerical worker (one year), then assistant field manager (five years), and service officer (ten years). I left because there was a difference between my hopes and company policy and because I had some difficulties with my boss. In 1981 I joined this firm as a branch sales manager. I was promoted in two years to branch office manager and two years later to assistant manager of the sales administration section. After working at this position for four years, I was made department manager.

These descriptions of external managerial careers fit those typical of core "lifetime" employees of Japanese firms and of Japanese managers who have ventured or been pushed into the non-Japanese firm labor market (Wakabayashi, Graen, Graen, & Graen, 1988; Abegglen & Stalk, 1985). Regardless of employer, most had worked for a very small number of organizations and remained in each position three to five years. Lateral transfers occurred more often than promotions in Japanese organizations, compared to U.S. Japanese subsidiaries. The question for the future of these managers is whether such stable patterns can persist.

To gain an understanding of how Japanese managers interpret these career patterns, we turn to their internal career beliefs and attitudes. These include work values or ultimate career goals, as well as plans, strategies, and satisfaction.

Internal Careers

Line managers were asked their opinions and beliefs about four key aspects of their careers—their career plans, career goals, career tactics, and career satisfaction. In each case, open-ended questions gave participants an opportunity to respond in their own words, while structured questions were used to relate their beliefs to beliefs found in other studies and other countries.

Career Plans, Goals, and Beliefs. Very early in the interviews, managers were asked to "Briefly describe any plans you have for your career." The following was a typical response:

I'm twenty-three now, by my early fifties I want to be a member of the board; and after fifty-five I want to try to actualize my own dream to buy a yacht and drift in the sea with nothing to do, so I will prepare for this in my early forties. Also after retirement, I seek to do some kind of volunteer activities.

Others responded more briefly: "Before, I thought I wanted to have my own independent company. Now I want to be a manager who can do all-round business at my present company"; "My plans are to be transferred to a branch office. I want to transfer so I can live with my family"; "I have no exact plan, but if I had a chance to get a job that could use my ability, I would like the challenge"; and "I just want to take life as it is."

When asked how much they had thought about their career before the interview, the mean response was 2.91 on a scale of 1 (not at all) to 5 (a great deal). When asked how specific their plans for their future work life were, three people reported no plans at all. The mean response was 2.57 on a scale of 1 (Very General) to 5 (Very Specific). Eight people (8.7%) reported that they lived their work lives day by day and the same number planned one year or less into the future. Most plans (43.5%) extended two to five years into the future.

Those who worked for Japanese firms were less likely than those working for U.S. firms to believe that the firm had specific plans for their future. All believed it was equally likely or unlikely that their own career plans matched any plans the organization had for their future.

Respondents were asked about their career goals when they first entered the labor force, as well as their contemporary career goals and criteria for career success. One-quarter of all Japanese managers reported no specific career aspirations when they entered the labor force. The only aspiration reported by slightly more than 10 percent was to use their skills or education. Their current criteria for career success were most commonly to have a good income, to achieve challenging objectives, to contribute to their companies, to gain esteem or prestige, and to be satisfied with the careers they experienced (each mentioned by about 10 percent). Representative responses were as follows: "I want to improve my private life, and the public and company environment. I want to continue to have a well-balanced working life"; and "For the long-term, self-development, growth are my goals; but right now my first priority is to do my present job better."

The structured career goals question was phrased as follows: People work for many different reasons, which we could call long-term career goals. Thinking about all of the jobs you will have in your work life, how important is it that your work life contain each of the following? Respondents were asked to rate each of twenty-three goals (1 = of little importance, 3 = moderately important, 5 = extremely important), and then were asked to pick their top five to rank order and to select one that was their immediate short-term goal. Results of the importance ratings are shown in Table 5.2.

Goals with a mean rating exceeding 4 (i.e., very important) included earning a good income, creativity, friendship, achievement of challenges, and having meaningful or interesting work. Japanese managers employed in Japanese firms rated friendship, contributing to their society, and general well-being as significantly more important than did Japanese managers employed by Japanese subsidiaries of U.S. firms.

When managers were asked to rank their top five goals, meaningful or interesting work was most often selected as number one (16%) and was

Table 5.2

Importance of Career Goals and Satisfaction with Attaining Organizational Career Goals among Japanese Line Managers

Goals	Employed in U.S. Firms (n-30)		Employed in Japanese Firms (n-66)	
	Importance[a]	Satisfaction[b]	Importance	Satisfaction
Income	4.31	3.20	3.98	3.09
Prestige	3.69	3.20	3.88	3.23
Power	3.38	3.13	3.21	2.98
Skills	4.07	3.37	3.88	3.27
Creativity	3.79	3.12	4.09	3.39
Fun	3.76	2.87	4.06	3.31[d]
Working hours	3.39	3.24	3.09	3.15
Friendship	3.68	3.13	4.21[c]	3.50[d]
Promotions	3.43	3.30	3.70	3.39
Variety	3.14	3.03	3.12	3.44[d]
Autonomy	3.50	3.39	3.80	3.36
Achievement	3.90	3.10	4.12	3.39
Location	3.43	3.37	3.36	3.30
Contribution to the firm	3.72	3.43	3.70	3.38
Contribution to society	3.03	3.10	3.86[c]	3.09
Contribution to family	3.86	3.17	3.95	3.32
Security	3.45	2.70	3.68	3.83[d]
Working conditions	3.59	3.07	3.73	3.31
Keeping busy	2.75	2.90	2.80	2.89
Fringe benefits	3.27	2.70	3.11	3.12[d]
Meaningful work	4.21	3.30	4.13	3.35
Growth	4.10	3.27	3.92	3.29
Well being	3.43	3.03	4.11[c]	3.21

a. 1 = very unimportant, 5 = very important.
b. 1 = very dissatisfied, 5 = very satisfied.
c. Significantly different career goal importance, $p \leq .05$.
d. Significantly different career goal satisfaction, $p \leq .05$.

included in their top five by 43 percent of all Japanese managers. Meaningful work was selected by 15 percent as their immediate short-term goal, important enough to influence them to change their jobs. Income was selected by 20 percent as their most important short-term goal.

Personal and work values measured by other scholars support these results. For example, internal values (such as meaningful work, well-being, and achievement) and positive personal relationships were highly valued by Japanese managers and trainers in 1979 and 1985 in one longitudinal study (Adams, Peterson, & Schwind, 1987). The importance of income seems somewhat stronger in the present study, but changing economic fortunes in Japan may have made this value more salient.

Respondents were also asked, How satisfied are you that this organization provides you with each of the following opportunities or rewards? (1 = Very Dissatisfied, 5 = Very Satisfied). The items were the same ones used to evaluate career goals. These responses also are shown in Table 5.2. Most employees were quite satisfied with all aspects of their organizational rewards. Japanese managers working for U.S. firms were less satisfied with fun, friendship, security, variety, and fringe benefit rewards than those working for Japanese firms.

Career Tactics or Processes. Line managers also were asked, What, if anything, are you doing to have the kind of work life or career you want? That is, do you have any career tactics? Fourteen respondents did not answer this open-ended question, and another twenty-eight answered "none." For those who reported career tactics (66% of the sample), the most common responses were doing their current job well (13.5%), learning more (10.4%), or getting more education (9.4%). One respondent said, "I want to be an administrative division manager and participate in management. I work hard, but I don't know how to get there."

When asked if anything or anyone might prevent or block them from having the careers they wanted, more than one-third could foresee no blocks (38%). Among the blocks mentioned, company policies were most common (16.7%), followed by their own skills or performance (7%). For example, one respondent said, "The way this company climate and the status quo is and my age is, I cannot see into the next year. I cannot predict, so this year I will do my best." The most common people to help them achieve their career goals were supervisors (19%) and friends and co-workers (21%).

The structured question about career tactics asked, In order to reach your career goals or to have the kind of work life you want, how likely are you to do each of the following things? (1 = very unlikely, 5 = very likely). This was followed by thirty-six items, including power and influence strategies, career strategies, and responses suggested by Asian social scientists. Results are reported in Table 5.3. Tactics rated as extremely likely (mean greater than 4.0) included doing their current job well and conforming to what is expected. Also, learning more was ranked in the top five by 66 percent of the sample.

There were many significant tactical differences between Japanese managers employed by Japanese and U.S. firms. Those working for Japanese firms were more likely to ask for what they wanted, exchange favors, get help from their families, gain more control over their jobs, change the way they thought about their jobs, create a network, or start their own firms. Japanese managers employed in U.S. Japanese subsidiaries were more likely to work long hours, do their current jobs well, do things others would notice, do what their supervisors desired, or get a job in a new

Table 5.3
Career Tactics of Japanese Line Managers

Tactics	Employed in U.S. Firms (n = 30)	Employed in Japanese Firms (n = 66)
Give extra effort[1]	4.00	3.95
Work long hours	2.90	2.04*
Do my job well	4.41	3.85*
Do things others notice	3.62	3.06*
Do what my boss wants	3.83	3.35*
Act humble	3.17	3.41
Assertively ask	2.83	4.11*
Exchange favors	3.10	3.77*
Threaten to leave	1.62	1.39
Ask for help	2.90	2.57
Develop an action plan	3.63	3.27
Get help from friends	3.13	2.94
Give loyalty to firm	3.57	2.83*
Give loyalty to supervisor	3.23	2.88
Learn more	4.23	4.27
Get more education	3.77	3.88
Develop subordinate rapport	3.72	3.65
Do better than peers	3.65	3.44
Become indispensable	3.90	3.80
Gain access to information	3.63	3.85
Conform to firm norms	3.80	4.04
Get help from my family	1.87	2.32*
Get help from gods	1.33	1.27
Change my family plans	1.67	2.01
Transfer to a different job	2.37	2.52
Get a job in a new organization	2.43	1.94*
Get a second job	1.83	1.88
Create a new job	2.80	2.94
Get more control of my job	2.50	3.53*
Change my own thinking	2.67	3.32*
Create a network	3.23	3.74*
Start my own firm	1.90	2.39*
Get others to recognize my work	2.10	1.97
Leave it to fate	2.07	1.42*
Tell my boss	2.69	2.38
Get career guidance	2.57	2.32

Note: 1 = Very unlikely to do, 5 = very likely to do.
*Significantly different, $p \leq .05$.

organization to have the careers they desired. They were also more likely to leave their careers to fate, although this was an uncommon strategy for most managers. Other very uncommon things to do included threatening to leave the organization and getting help from God or other deities.

When asked how likely it would be that they could get a job in another company, Japanese managers in Japanese firms reported a very low probability, whereas Japanese managers employed in U.S. firms, many of whom who had moved at least once from a Japanese firm to their present firm, were more optimistic.

When asked why they could not get a better job in another firm, a manager replied, "The characteristics of my job make it hard for me to change (I am a *Kacho* section manager, not a specialist who can change more easily)." Another response was, "I am now forty-one years old. I will have no security for my compensation if I change."

The U.S.-employed managers were a little more optimistic about the ease of getting a different job inside their firms that was equal to or better than their past jobs. One manager replied, "This company has good personnel policies, and if I want to change it is possible." Another said, "If a person has special talents (or) skills, they can change jobs here, if that skill can be used in the company."

Recognizing that careers are shaped not only by individual plans but also by external forces, we asked managers to rate a series of twenty-nine factors for how much influence or control each might have over the next job they would have. If they did not expect to have another job in their work lives, they could use their present jobs as an example. The factors were loosely categorized as organizational, job-related, family, public policy, personal skill or experience, and personal plans and characteristics. By far the most influential were current and future job characteristics and the firm's reputation, policy, and growth. When asked to rank the top five, company growth potential was ranked by 61 percent in their top five and ranked number one by 12 percent. The value of the job was in the top five for 57 percent and ranked number one by 24 percent. There were few differences in career control factors by type of employing firm, but spouses, parents, and spiritual counselors were seen as more influential for those employed by Japanese firms. Grades and personal career plans were rated as more influential by Japanese managers employed by U.S. firms.

Individual Career Outcomes. In addition to having plans, goals, and strategies for shaping their careers, most people have positive or negative feelings about their work lives and about other aspects of their lives. Specific satisfaction with achieving career goals was reported in Table 5.2. More general affective responses were discussed in open-ended questions. Only three Japanese managers reported bad or negative general feelings about their careers. Another 14 percent were neutral, 30 percent had mixed feelings, and 50 percent reported generally positive feelings about their careers. When asked, In general, how satisfied are you with meeting your career goals so far in your life? (1 = very dissatisfied, 5 = very satisfied), the majority responded by selecting 3 (40%) or 4 (44%); a parallel question about life satisfaction had essentially the same results (3 = 42%; 4 = 45%). Those working for U.S. firms were significantly more satisfied with their careers than those employed by Japanese firms (x_J = 3.31; $x_{U.S.}$ = 3.73; $p \leq .05$).

The close relationship between career satisfaction and life satisfaction may have occurred because most managers said that work was one of the most important things in their total lives ($x_{imp.}$ = 4.37), confirming earlier reports of the importance of work among Japanese people (Tung, 1984). Japanese managers were somewhat less optimistic but still positive when asked to estimate how likely they were to achieve career success, reflecting a normal distribution from 0 to 100 percent probability of success. Some of these positive feelings may be attributed to their beliefs that they were effective in their jobs (x = 3.36) and would be rewarded for doing a good job (x = 3.41; 1 = very unlikely, and 5 = very likely).

When managers were asked how they combined work and the other aspects of their lives (like their families), most managers said they tried to separate these parts of their lives, but a few had more specific plans for integration of different parts of their lives: "I forget about work at private times"; "Both are very important"; and "I did it case by case" were typical responses. One manager responded: "Before marriage and childbirth, I got the chance to separate work and private life, but now our child is older, and he has a lot of homework. I leave that to my wife and if my wife needs me, I will do family work." This separation of family from work life and the separation of men and women's roles were frequently given as reasons why the managers could live very busy lives and have positive life and work satisfaction.

CONCLUSIONS AND IMPLICATIONS

In summary, the Japanese line managers in this sample resembled stereotypical Japanese salarymen in external careers but revealed interesting details of their internal career beliefs not usually reported in the English literature on Japan. They also revealed some differences if employed in a U.S. rather than a Japanese firm. These middle-aged men employed in Japanese service or manufacturing organizations had traditional careers of many lateral transfers and two or three promotions in one firm. Japanese employees of U.S. firms had similar careers but fewer transfers, more promotions, and had been employed in two or more firms.

Work was a central part of their lives, and they were reasonably satisfied with their careers so far. They had very general career plans extending two to five years into the future. Intrinsic rewards such as meaning, creativity, challenge, friendship, and social contribution were their most important long-term goals, but income was an equally important short-term goal.

In order to achieve these career goals, Japanese managers working for Japanese firms were using general job performance and conformity, while those working for U.S. firms were more likely to try to please supervisors or to leave the firm. Organizational policies most often stood in the way of individual career achievement, while friends, families, and supervisors most often provided help in attaining their career goals.

Japanese employees working for U.S. firms were influenced by differences in organizational policies related to fringe benefits and job security. These policies decreased their career satisfaction and created substantial conflict for the Japanese human resources managers of the U.S. firms.

Implications for Organizations

In addition to the characteristics of Japanese managers that sounded familiar from other descriptions, these data offered a few different insights that might influence organizational responses when firms from other nations operate in the Japanese national context. Regardless of employment setting, most Japanese managers valued learning and having meaningful work, and would use further education to try to achieve the kinds of careers they desired. However, they perceived significant organizational policy barriers to doing so.

The future challenge for any firm operating in a slower Japanese economic context with an aging workforce is to enable all managers to feel that the jobs they do are meaningful, creative, interesting, and challenging. Since employees are very willing to learn new skills to be able to do such jobs well, and since status and promotion are not highly valued career goals, job redesign rather than promotion might be considered for improving managerial positions. Japanese businesses have a strong tradition of enriched jobs for manufacturing employees that might be applied in new ways to managerial positions that have become routine or unchallenging.

One of the most interesting incongruities of Japanese managers employed in Japanese firms is that the managers value creativity but would use conformity to have the careers they want. Concerns about whether traditional Japanese education and social norms suppress creativity is sometimes expressed in popular press and private conversation. The desire to express creativity in the workplace is strong in the managers who were involved in this study. The challenge is for Japanese organizations to create a normative structure where creativity in management is valued and rewarded in a culture that values uncertainty avoidance (which may be threatened by creativity).

The challenge for non-Japanese firms operating in Japan with Japanese employees is to create a "good reputation" so that the most talented Japanese employees would desire to enter, work hard for, and remain with the firm. According to these Japanese managers, to have a good reputation a U.S. firm would need to offer high growth potential, challenging jobs, security, and fringe benefits more in line with Japanese firms. Many U.S. firms would like to offer this ideal to employees, but often do not because of perceived costs. Adopting policies more in line with the Japanese cultural context may reduce long-term turnover costs and make this a less expensive alternative than it would appear to be at first analysis. Japanese employees working for U.S. firms were much more likely than employees of Japanese firms to perceive that equal or better jobs would be available if they looked for them and were more likely to leave if dissatisfied.

Because socialization to an organizational culture different from the employees' national culture is a long and expensive process, funds U.S. firms spend providing desirable work settings might be considered an investment rather than an unwanted cost, especially if this expenditure resulted in a core of employees knowledgeable about both the national business context and the unique organizational culture and needs.

Because Japanese firms often wish to send older or less productive managers to other affiliated firms, any investment made in order to become attractive to the *best* Japanese managers rather than being the resting place for Japanese-firm "cast-offs" has the potential for substantial long-term rewards for U.S. firms operating in Japan.

Future Challenges

Although these are only a few of the lessons which might be drawn from these data, they provide a starting place for greater intercultural understanding and a basic foundation for future research on Japanese careers. Challenges left for future research include examining careers of women; careers of nonmanagerial employees; careers of Japanese workers in other non-Japanese settings; careers of Japanese workers employed by Japanese firms but located outside of Japan; and postretirement careers of older workers. Hopefully, this initial step provides a framework for shaping these studies and provides basic data useful for comparison to a wide variety of careers in other contexts.

Finally, in recent years much debate has arisen over the extent to which many of the attitudes and behaviors identified in this study remain typical of Japanese firms and their employees. Incidents of deregulation and privatization in key industry sectors, increases in labor mobility rates, corporate downsizing, and organizational restructuring have been cited as evidence that the Japanese management system is in a state of transition.

We believe that such a conclusion is premature. Whether such actions constitute a fundamental, lasting shift or a short-term response to economic exigencies remains unclear. Our own findings suggest that, even if significant changes are underway, traditional approaches are still firmly entrenched in the minds of Japanese middle managers. As a result, this study provides a marker against which future shifts in the career-related thoughts and behaviors of Japanese managers can be measured.

REFERENCES

Abegglen, J., & Stalk, G., Jr. (1985). *Kaisha: The Japanese corporation*. New York: Basic Books.

Adams, R. J., Peterson, R. B., & Schwind, H. P. (1987). *Personal values of Japanese managers and trainees in a changing competitive system*. Paper presented at the Academy of Management annual meeting, New Orleans, LA.

Aoto, Y., Fukuzawa, S., Hoyoshi, R., & Yage, H. (1988). *Nipon the land and its people*. Translated by Richard Foster. Tokyo: Nipon Steel HRD Co. Ltd.

Beck, J. C., & Beck, M. N. (1994). *The change of a lifetime: Employment patterns among Japan's managerial elites*. Honolulu, HI: University of Hawaii Press.

Friedman, D. (1988). *The misunderstood miracle: Industrial development and political change in Japan*. Ithaca, NY: Cornell University Press.

Hofstede, G. (1981). *Culture's consequences*. Beverly Hills, CA: Sage.

Japanese Ministry of Education. (1994). *Basic school statistics*. Tokyo: the Ministry.

Japanese Ministry of Labor (1995). *Status quo of working women* (p. 62). Tokyo: the Ministry.

Keizai Koho Center. (1995). *Japan 1995: An international comparison*. Tokyo: Taiheisha.

Ogawa, N., Jones, G. W., & Williamson, J. G. (Eds., 1993). *Human resources in development along the Asia-Pacific Rim*. New York: Oxford University Press.

Ouchi, W. G. (1981). *Theory Z: How American business can meet the Japanese challenge*. Reading, MA: Addison-Wesley.

Ouchi, W. G., & Johnson, J. B. (1978). Types of organizational control and their relationship to emotional well-being. *Administrative Science Quarterly, 24*, 220–241.

Ozawa, K. (1995). Ambivalence in Asia. *Japanese Update, 44*, 18–19.

Pucik, V. (1984). White-collar human resources in large Japanese manufacturing firms. *Human Resource Management, 23*, 257–276.

Reischauer, E. O., & Craig, A. M. (1978). *Japan: Tradition and transformation*. New York: Houghton-Mifflin.

Triandis, H. C., Bontempo, R., Villareal, M. J., Asai, M., & Lucca, N. (1988). Individualism and collectivism: Cross-cultural perspectives on self-ingroups relations. *Journal of Personality and Social Psychology, 54*(2), 323–338.

Tung, R. L. (1984). *Key to Japan's economic strength: Human power*. Lexington, MA: Lexington Books.

United Nations. (1993). *International trade statistics yearbook*. New York: United Nations.

Wakabayashi, M., & Graen, G. B. (1984). The Japanese career progress study: A 7-year followup. *Journal of Applied Psychology, 69*(4), 603–614.

Wakabayashi, M., Graen, G. B., Graen, M., & Graen, M. (1988). Japanese management progress: Mobility into middle management. *Journal of Applied Psychology, 73*(2), 217–227.

Watanabe, T., & Holley, D. (1996, August 14). Japanese jolted by demands of the future. *Los Angeles Times*, pp. 1, 15–16.

Wood, C. (1994). *The end of Japan Inc.* New York: Simon and Schuster.

Yeh, R. S., & Phatak, A. (1987). *Human resource management of U.S. and Japanese subsidiaries in Taiwan*. Paper presented at the Academy of Management annual meeting, New Orleans, LA.

CHAPTER SIX

Individualism and Collectivism in Asian Managers' Careers

Rey-Yeh Lin

In the past two decades, East Asia has shown rapid economic development, especially in Hong Kong, Japan, Singapore, and Taiwan. The economic success in these countries has placed pressure on the global development of many Western countries. Many researchers (Hicks & Redding, 1983; Hofheinz & Calder, 1982; Redding, 1990) have identified the factors that have contributed to the accomplishments of these Asian countries. They then attempt to distinguish the differences between Eastern and Western management philosophies and try to absorb the quintessence of the Eastern management to increase the efficiency of the Western management. In this process, they find that many distinctions between Eastern and Western management styles are rooted in cultural differences. These cultural differences not only can affect people's social life but also their work behavior. Since many U.S. multinational corporations have been expanding their investments in East Asia, it would be helpful to developing suitable management strategies for workers from different cultural backgrounds to understand how cultural values affect their work demeanor.

The research presented here examines the relationship between career planning processes and cultural values among managers from the United States, Hong Kong, Japan, Singapore, and Taiwan. Two major career planning processes—selecting career goals and tactics—are investigated here. According to Gould's (1979) career planning model, the first step of individual career planning is setting one's career goals. The goals then will direct an individual's efforts to achieve his or her goals. In order to achieve career goals, the individual will develop certain career tactics to enhance his or her career performance. Research has indicated that matching individual career plans and organizational career management can increase employees' satisfaction with the organization and decrease their desire to leave the organization (Granrose & Portwood, 1987). In order to achieve a match, it is necessary for organizations to understand the career goals and tactics of their employees from different cultures. The organizations can then design proper career management policies and career paths for different employees. In addition, Burke (1991) finds that in a diverse organization, supporting the career goals of minorities not only can improve the performance of the minorities but also can have benefits for the majority and for the organization as well. Hence, understanding the career goals and tactics of employees from different cultures is important.

People are deeply influenced by the cultural values and norms they hold. Among all the cultural differences, individualism–collectivism has been viewed "as one of the most important dimensions of variation across the cultures of the world" (Meindl, Hunt, & Lee, 1989). It has been found to be related to individual values, social systems, economic development, and cognitive differentiation (Triandis, McCusker, & Hui, 1990). Many studies have found that this cultural difference exists consistently between the United States and East Asian cultures, including Hong Kong, Japan, Singapore, and Taiwan (e.g., Hofstede, 1980; Hofstede & Bond, 1984; Hui, 1988; Meindl, Hunt, Lee, & Elizur, 1986; Shenkar & Ronen, 1987; Yamaguchi, 1994). This research hypothesizes that differences in individualism–collectivism values are related to choosing different career goals and tactics for U.S., Hong Kong, Japanese, Singaporean, and Taiwanese managers.

INDIVIDUALISM AND COLLECTIVISM

The construct of individualism–collectivism is multidimensional. Several researchers have provided different definitions of the construct. Among them, Triandis, Leung, Villareal, and Clark (1985) give the clearest comparison of individualism and collectivism. According to their definition, in collectivist cultures, people are susceptible to the expectations and needs of their ingroup. Therefore, individuals' behavior is highly regulated by their ingroup norms. Collectivists also tend to believe that ingroup goals are more important than personal goals. When there is a conflict between individual goals and ingroup goals, they will choose to fulfill ingroup goals first.

Harmony is another attribute of collectivist cultures. People in the same group are supposed to have homogeneous opinions; hence, harmony can be maintained among ingroup members. Furthermore, face-saving is important in collectivist cultures. Collectivists care about whether their behavior would be a shame to their ingroup members. They also avoid indicating other people's mistakes in public, so other people would not feel that they have lost face. Because individuals are so close to their ingroups, they feel they have a shared fate and are highly interdependent.

On the other hand, in individualistic cultures, people's behavior is regulated by their individual norms. Although individualists also form certain ingroups, they do not believe that they have a common fate with their ingroup members. Individualists consider themselves independent, separate individuals; hence, they are less likely to conform to the expectations of others. When group goals are conflicting with personal goals, it is common for individualists to pursue their personal goals. In addition, seeking personal identity is highly valued in individualistic cultures (Waterman, 1984). In individualistic cultures, confrontation with others within an ingroup is acceptable. Personal achievement, pleasure, and competition are all highly valued.

The individualism–collectivism construct reflects values and norms emphasized in different cultures (Hofstede, 1980; Triandis, 1980). In Hofstede's (1980) cross-cultural study, individualism–collectivism is considered one of the work-related value dimensions and can influence workers to choose different work goals. Other researchers view individualism–collectivism as a cultural value that is linked with other work-related values (Meindl, Hunt, & Lee, 1989; Schwartz & Bilsky, 1987; the Chinese Culture Connection, 1987; Triandis, McCusker, & Hui, 1990). Several work-related values have been related to the construct of individualism––collectivism. In Schwartz and Bilsky's (1987) research, self-direction (sense of accomplishment, imaginative, intellectual), achievement (ambitious, seeking recognition, capable), and enjoying life (comfortable life, pleasure, happiness) correspond to individualism. Prosocial behavior (helpful, forgiving), conformity (obedient, polite, clean), and security (national security, world of peace, and harmony) are found to be related to collectivism. Meindl, Hunt, and Lee (1989) collected data from the United States, PRC, Taiwan, Korea, and Hong Kong to analyze the relationship between individualism-collectivism and work values. They found that the United States and PRC had the lowest and highest scores on the collectivism dimension, respectively. The rest of the countries were clustered in the middle. They measured twenty-four work values and found that 84.09 percent of the total variance of these values could be explained by the dimension of individualism–collectivism. Among these nations, valuing society, security, conditions, benefits, and ability are the most discriminating values. In addition, the results of Triandis, McCusker, and Hui's (1990) research indicate that collectivist values include social order, self-discipline, social recognition, being humble, honoring parents and elders, accepting one's position in life, and preserving public image. Individualists believe that equality, freedom, an exciting life, a varied life, and enjoying life are more important.

Summarizing these findings, collectivists and individualists hold two different sets of values. Collectivists tend to believe that the values of contribution to society, humility, conformity, security, family, and preserving public image are more important. On the other hand, individualists view the values of personal achievement, ambition, competition, freedom, benefits, and enjoying life as important. The study described in this chapter examines how these different values are reflected in career goal setting and the career tactics selected by managers to achieve these goals.

CAREER GOALS AND TACTICS

Career goals are the objectives that individuals expect to achieve in the series of jobs in their lives. Career tactics are the strategies or methods that individuals choose to increase the possibility of achieving their career goals. Research on individual career planning models (Gould, 1979; Hall, 1971) has provided evidence that once an individual selects his or her career goals, he or she will adopt certain tactics to achieve these goals. Aryee and Debrah (1993) have found a similar relationship between career goals and tactics among Chinese workers. Because values reflect what is important to an individual, the selection of career goals and tactics is expected to be influenced by individualism–collectivism values.

This research anticipates that managers from the United States, Hong Kong, Japan, Singapore, and Taiwan will choose different career goals and career tactics because they hold different cultural values regarding individualism–collectivism. It is important for multinational corporations to recognize these differences in order to develop various career management polices for their employees from different cultures.

HYPOTHESES

The degree of individualism–collectivism can be related to many factors. In this study, ethnicity, sex, age, and firm type are taken into account when comparing how managers in the United States, Hong Kong, Japan, Singapore, and Taiwan choose their career goals and tactics.

Ethnicity

During the 1960s and 1970s, Hofstede used survey methods to collect data from more than fifty countries. The results of his survey indicate that the United States is ranked highest in individualism. On the opposite end,

East Asian countries such as Japan, Hong Kong, Singapore, and Taiwan are low in this dimension. Other researchers have found the same results using similar and different methods (Hofstede & Bond, 1984; Hui, 1988; Triandis, McCusker, & Hui, 1990; Wheeler, Reis, & Bond, 1989; Yamaguchi, 1994).

Among these East Asian countries, Hong Kong, Singapore, and Taiwan are mainly composed of ethnic Chinese. Although Japan is different from these Asian countries in race, the Japanese are profoundly influenced by Confucianism. By closely examining the concepts of Confucianism, researchers (Hofheinz & Calder, 1982; Kahn & Pepper, 1979; Yu & Yang, 1994) have agreed that they correspond to collectivist values. Confucianism emphasizes the values of obedience to authority and commitment to the solidarity, harmony, and norms of the group. The influence of Confucianism motivates Chinese and Japanese workers to pursue social-oriented achievement (Yu & Yang, 1994). Therefore, it is reasonable to expect that Chinese and Japanese managers will tend to value the collectivist career goals as more important than those that are individualistic.

In the late 1950s, McClelland, Atkinson, Russel, and Lowell (1958) pointed out that Western society stresses individual success. Literature (Hofstede, 1980; Hofstede & Bond, 1984; Wheeler, Reis, & Bond, 1989) also shows that the United States is dominated by individualism. Pursuing individual success is expected to be reflected in career goal setting among U.S. managers. They will be more likely to consider individualistic career goals more valuable than collectivist career goals.

H1a: U.S. managers will consider individualistic career goals more important than will Chinese and Japanese managers.

H1b: Chinese and Japanese managers will consider collectivist career goals more important than will U.S. managers.

Evidence shows that individualism–collectivism values are related to behavior (Triandis, 1980). Certain patterns of behavior are considered to be more appropriate in individualistic cultures than in collectivist cultures. In individualistic cultures, competition and self-identity are valued (Triandis, Bontempo, Villareal, Asai, & Lucca, 1988; Waterman, 1984). Therefore, individualists are more likely to use assertive tactics (e.g., to ask what they want directly) to achieve their goals. Since U.S. managers grow up in an individualistic society, they will believe that by using individualistic career tactics they will be more likely to achieve their goals than by adopting collectivist career tactics.

On the other hand, collectivist cultures emphasize the values of humility and conformity, and collectivist individuals are intimate with members of their ingroups. Therefore, collectivists are more likely to use collaborative tactics such as acting humble and conforming to a group norm. It is expected that Chinese and Japanese managers will believe that by employing collectivist career tactics they are more likely to reach their career goals than by applying individualistic career tactics.

H2a: U.S. managers will rank individualistic career tactics as more important than will Chinese and Japanese managers.

H2b: Chinese and Japanese managers will rank collectivist tactics as more important than will U.S. managers.

Gender

Males and females tend to hold different notions of self. Lykes (1985), summarizing preliminary research, found that males emphasize autonomy, separation, and independence more than females. Gire and Carment (1983) collected data by using a modified version of Hui's individualism–collectivism scale. They found that when dealing with disputes, males are likely to use threats, whereas females prefer negotiation. In Eagly's (1987) study, females in most societies are expected to place family and children above their individual goals. These findings support a relation between individualism–collectivism and sex role norms.

Early research has found that males and females tend to consider different aspects of jobs important (Bartol, 1976; Manhardt, 1972). Males are concerned with their advancement and earnings. On the other hand, females often emphasize the importance of relationships with their co-workers and superiors. Knight and Dubro (1984) collected data from 100 undergraduates and found that males were less likely to emphasize group enhancement and more likely to consider superiority important. Therefore, it is plausible that female managers in both collectivist and individualistic societies will tend to consider collectivist career goals and tactics more valuable and will be less favorable about individualistic career goals and tactics than male managers.

H3: For managers from Chinese, Japanese, and U.S. communities, female managers will be more likely than male managers to consider collectivist career goals and tactics more important than individualistic career goals and tactics.

Age

There has been a national shift from collectivism to individualism in many parts of the world in the past thirty years. Affluence is the major determinant of the shift (Triandis, 1989). In Hofstede's (1980) research, individualism is correlated ($r = .80$) with gross national product per capita. Because of the rapid economic development in Hong Kong, Japan, Singapore, and Taiwan, people in these countries are becoming more affluent. It is expected that younger people who grew up in more affluent East Asian societies will be more individualistic than older people in those societies. Forty-five is the age selected as a cutoff point for differentiating the younger and older generations due to the fact that the rapid economic growth in these countries occurred in the past twenty years.

H4: Chinese and Japanese managers who are under forty-five years old will have higher scores on items of individualistic career goals and tactics than those who are above forty-five. Chinese and Japanese managers who are under forty-five years old will have lower scores on items of collectivist career goals and tactics than those who are above forty-five.

Firm Type

Some research has found that work-related values can be influenced by both culture and business environments (Child, 1981; Beres & Portwood, 1981; Ronen, 1986). As U.S. firms expand their enterprises abroad, they bring their management systems with them. Since individualism is deeply rooted in U.S. culture, it is likely that U.S. firms in Asia will place more emphasis on individualistic values than will non-U.S. firms. As a result, Chinese and Japanese managers who work for U.S. firms will be more likely to adopt beliefs and behaviors related to individualistic work values.

H5: Chinese and Japanese managers working for U.S. firms will rate individualistic career goals and tactics as more important than will Chinese and Japanese managers working for non-U.S. firms.

RESEARCH DESIGN AND METHODS

Participants and Sampling

Firms in Hong Kong, Japan, Singapore, Taiwan, and the United States were sampled according to three criteria: (1) They had more than 100 employees; (2) they were U.S. or Asian corporations; and (3) they were selected from petrochemical, manufacturing, financial services, or government sectors.

The human resources managers of these firms were asked to choose a sample of managers that represented all managerial levels and functional departments of the companies and included all major ethnic groups of the country. The managers who were chosen had to have at least one year of work experience and had to have been working in their current companies for six months or more. The whole sample included 202 Chinese managers (including 71 Hong Kong managers, 29 Singaporean managers, and 102 Taiwanese managers), 89 Japanese managers, and 65 U.S. managers. There were 35 female Chinese managers, 5 female Japanese managers, and 11 female U.S. managers.

Procedure

Questionnaires were distributed to the managers by the data collectors and human resources managers. The line managers were told that there were no right or wrong answers, and they should respond according to how they felt about each item. They also had an opportunity to ask investigators questions about the questionnaires and were assured of their confidentiality. Each of the managers was given the opportunity to participate in an interview, and about half of them did. The purpose of the interviews was to question the managers about their incomplete or unclear answers and to collect qualitative data about their career choices.

Measures

The independent variables included ethnicity, gender, age, and firm type. Each independent variable was measured by one item. The dependent variables were individualistic career goals, collectivist career goals, individualistic career tactics, and collectivist career tactics. Eight career goal items and twenty-one career tactic items were examined to construct the measures of individualistic career goals, collectivist career goals, individualistic career tactics, and collectivist career tactics.

Independent Variables.   Ethnicity (U.S. versus Japanese versus Chinese [Hong Kong, Singapore, and Taiwan]), gender, and age variables were all measured by one item each. The questions were as follows: What is your ethnic or racial group?; What is your gender?; and In what year were you born? Firm type (U.S. vs. non-U.S.) was taken from archival records. Managers from Hong Kong, Japan, and Taiwan were working for either U.S. or non-U.S. firms. U.S. and Singaporean managers were all working for U.S. firms.

Dependent Variables.   Eight items measured career goals. These items were selected from the studies of Hofstede (1980) and MOW (1987) and adapted for Asia with additions from Singaporean scholars at the National University of Singapore. Responses to each career goal item were made on a five-point scale (1 = of little importance and 5 = very important). The respondents were asked to decide how important it was that their work life contain each of the career goal items. The four items measuring individualistic career goals were: a good income, esteem or prestige, advancement or promotions, and power and influence. The four items measuring collectivist career goals were good relationships/friendship; contributing to your company; contributing to your society; and contributing to your family.

Career tactics were measured by twenty-one items from studies by Kipnis, Schmidt, and Wilkinson (1980), Falbo (1977), and other work on personal power and influence tactics. Ten of the items measured individualistic career tactics, such as do something important that others will notice; become indispensable; and do better than your peers. There were eleven items used to measure collectivist career tactics. Some examples are act humble or courteous toward your superiors; conform to what is expected; and show loyalty toward your organization. The respondents were asked to indicate how likely they were to use each of the tactics. These items were rated on a five-point scale (1 = very unlikely and 5 = very likely).

Reliability.   Principle components extraction with varimax rotation factor analysis was performed to extract the factors that measure individualistic career goals, collectivist career goals, individualistic career tactics, and collectivist career tactics. The career beliefs data were analyzed as a whole first. Then the data of the Chinese managers, Japanese managers, and U.S. managers were analyzed separately to see whether the managers from different countries defined individualism and collectivism differently.

The data were screened prior to this factor analysis. There was an absence of outliers, and the variables were factorable. After missing values were deleted by listwise method, there were 354 respondents for the career goal variables, 307 respondents for the individualistic career tactic variables, and 334 respondents for the collectivist career variables.

Two factors were extracted from the career goal variables. The results indicated that there was a similar loading structure whether the data were analyzed separately by ethnicity or together. Each factor included four variables. The first factor, which explained 33.4 percent of the total variance, was defined as the measure of individualistic career goals. The second factor was identified as the collectivist career goals, reflecting 20.7 percent of the total variance. The internal-consistency reliability of the individualistic career goals scale and the collectivist career goals scale were *alpha* = .71 and *alpha* = .70, respectively.

Factor analyses of the individualistic career tactic variables and the collectivist career tactic variables using the Chinese, Japanese, and U.S. data individually and collectively were undertaken. Although the loading structures for each group were not exactly the same, six items were selected from each of the individualistic career tactic variables and the collectivist career tactic variables to construct an individualistic career tactics scale and a collectivist career tactics scale based on the patterns of the loading structures. The coefficient alpha of the individualistic career tactics scale and the collectivist career tactics scale were both *alpha* = .70.

Data Analysis

MANOVA and Bonferroni *t*-tests were used to test the hypotheses. MANOVA was used to control experimentwise error rate with multiple dependent measures of collectivist and individualistic career goals and career tactics. When a significant effect was found in the multivariate analysis, a special contrast step MANOVA or Bonferroni t-test was performed to examine the differences between groups in the individual dependent variables. Before the hypothesis testing, data were screened to assure that the assumptions of these tests were not violated.

Because only the Hong Kong, Japanese, and Taiwanese data sets had managers working for U.S. or non-U.S. firms, the effect of firm type (two levels) was examined first to see if it was necessary to consider the effect of firm type when Hypotheses 1a, 1b, 2a, 2b, and 3 were tested. A MANOVA was performed; the independent variables were country (three levels—Hong Kong, Japan, and Taiwan) and firm type (two levels—U.S. firms, non-U.S. firms). When the multivariate tests of the main effect of firm type were not significant, $F_{df 4, 259} = 1.78, p < .14$, the effect of firm type was not considered when analyzing the effects of ethnicity and gender.

A MANOVA was performed to test the effects of ethnicity and gender simultaneously. When the multivariate tests of the main effect of ethnicity was significant, a special contrast MANOVA was employed to analyze the differences between responses from each Asian country and the U.S. responses for each dependent variable.

A third MANOVA was performed to examine the effect of age in the Asian countries. The independent variables were country (four levels—Hong Kong, Japan, Singapore, Taiwan) and age (two levels—under forty-five and above forty-five). When the multivariate tests of the main effect of country and age were significant, a Bonferroni t-test was conducted to examine the difference between different ages within each country in the individual dependent variables.

RESULTS

Ethnicity and Gender

A MANOVA with sequential adjustment for nonorthogonality was performed for the analysis of ethnicity and gender differences. The analysis of firm-type effect indicates that there was no difference between managers working for the U.S. firms and managers working for the non-U.S. firms in selecting career goals and career tactics. When the effects of ethnicity and gender were tested, the managers working for different firm types were grouped together. Order of entry of independent variables was ethnicity (five levels—United States, Hong Kong, Japan, Singapore, and Taiwan), then gender.

The results of the multivariate analysis indicate that the interaction effect between gender and ethnicity and the main effect of gender were not significant: gender x ethnicity, $F_{df 16, 1392} = 1.56, p < .21$; gender, $F_{df 4, 345} = 1.65, p < .15$. According to these findings, male and female managers did not rank the importance of individualistic and collectivist career goals and tactics differently. Therefore, Hypothesis 3 is not supported.

The multivariate test of ethnicity indicates that the effect of ethnicity was significant, $F_{df\,16,\,392} = 6.05$, $p < .001$. The impact of ethnicity on the individual dependent variables was significant for each variable: individualistic career goals, $F_{df\,4,\,348} = 8.42$, $p < .001$; collectivist career goals, $F = 5.79$, $p < .001$, individualistic career tactics, $F = 2.83$, $p < .05$; and collectivist career tactics, $F = 3.08$, $p < .05$. Therefore, a special contrast MANOVA was conducted to compare each Asian country with the United States in order to test Hypotheses 1a, 1b, 2a, and 2b.

The results of the multivariate tests of the comparison between each Asian country with the United States are shown in Table 6.1. Only the comparison between the Taiwanese managers and the U.S. managers was not significant. Therefore, the results of the univariate tests of the differences between the United States and each Asian country except for Taiwan were further examined.

The examination of the differences between the United States and each Asian country, excluding Taiwan, on each dependent variable are shown in Table 6.2. The comparison between the Japanese group and the U.S. group shows that they were significantly different in the collectivist goals, $F_{df\,1,\,348} = 6.88$, $p < .01$, and the collectivist career tactics, $F = 8.90$, $p < .01$. The U.S. managers tended to consider collectivist career goals as more important than the Japanese managers did. Also, they were more likely to use collectivist career tactics to achieve their goals than the Japanese managers. These findings were opposite of Hypotheses 1b and 2b. The comparison between the Hong Kong group and the U.S. group indicates that

Table 6.1
Multivariate Comparison of Individualistic–Collectivist Career Goals and Tactics

Compared Groups	Multivariate F	df	a level
Japan-U.S.	2.96**	4, 345	.020
Hong Kong-U.S.	9.56*	4, 251	.001
Singapore-U.S.	3.70*	4, 251	.001
Taiwan-U.S.	2.33	4, 345	.056

Note: Special contrast MANOVA multivariate test, $**p < .001$; $*p < .05$.

Table 6.2
Univariate Comparison of Asian and U.S. Career Goals and Tactics

Country	Mean		
Variables	Asian	U.S.	Univariate F
Japan-U.S.			
Career Goals			
Individualistic	3.70	3.72	.07
Collectivist	3.83	4.09	6.88**
Career Tactics			
Individualistic	3.41	3.51	1.33
Collectivist	3.24	3.51	8.90**
Hong Kong-U.S.			
Career Goals			
Individualistic	3.98	3.72	5.61*
Collectivist	3.64	4.09	
Career Tactics			
Individualistic	3.24	3.51	
Collectivist	3.38	3.51	2.21
Singapore-U.S.			
Career Goals			
Individualistic	3.95	3.72	2.73
Collectivist			
Career Tactics	4.12	4.09	.06
Individualistic	3.16	3.51	7.13**
Collectivist	3.41	3.51	.83

Note: Special contrast MANOVA univariate test, df = 1, 345. ***$p < .001$; **$p < .01$; *$p < .05$.

they were significantly different in individualistic career goals, $F = 5.61$, $p < .05$, collectivist career goals, $F = 16.75$, $p < .001$, and individualistic career tactics, $F = 7.22$, $p < .01$. The U.S. managers considered both the individualistic career goals and the collectivist career goals to be more important than the Hong Kong managers did. The U.S. managers were more likely to use individualistic career tactics to achieve their goals than the Hong Kong managers. These results support Hypotheses 1a and 2a.

The univariate tests show that there were no differences in rating the importance of individualistic and collectivist career goals between the Singaporean members and the U.S. group. The Singaporean mangers and the U.S. managers were significantly different in individualistic career tactics, $F = 7.13$, $p < .01$. The U.S. managers were more likely than the Singaporean managers to use individualistic career tactics to achieve their goals. Hypothesis 2a is supported by this finding.

Age

A MANOVA with sequential adjustment for nonorthogonality was performed for the analysis of age differences among the Asian managers. Order of entry of independent variables was country (Hong Kong, Japan, Singapore, and Taiwan), then age. The interaction between country and age was not significant. The multivariate tests indicate that there were significant effects of age, $F_{df\,4,276} = 10.17$, $p < .001$, and country, $F_{df\,12,834} = 6.12$, $p < .001$. The impact of age on the individual dependent variables indicated that there were significant effects in the individualistic career goals, $F_{df\,1,279} = 23.22$, $p < .001$, and the collectivist career tactics, $F = 5.15$, $p < .05$. Since these effects were significant, Bonferroni t-tests were used to determine significance of age within each country for the individualistic career goals and the collectivist career tactics.

Table 6.3 shows the results of the Bonferroni t-tests that were performed to compare the differences in individualistic career goals and collectivist career tactics between Asian managers who were less than forty-five years old and Asian managers who were more than forty-five years old within each country. For the Hong Kong group and the Singapore group, there were no significant effects in the individualistic career goals or in the collectivist career tactics. However, for the Taiwanese group, the mean for the managers who were less than forty-five years old was significantly higher than the mean for the managers who were more than forty-five years old in individualistic career goals, $t = 3.13$, $p < .05$. For the Japanese group, the older generation was more likely to use collectivist career tactics to achieve their goals than the younger generation, $t = -2.84$, $p < .05$. Therefore, Hypothesis 4 is partly supported by the Taiwanese group and Japanese group.

DISCUSSION

The purpose of this study is to examine whether individualism–collectivism is related to choosing different career goals and tactics among Asian and U.S. managers. The results of this study are not clearcut. The results of hypothesis testing indicate that the selection of individualistic and collectivist

Table 6.3
Effect of Age on Individualistic Career Goals and Collectivist Career Tactics for Asian Managers

Variables	Mean		t-value	df
	under 45	above 45		
Japan				
Individualistic career goals	3.77	3.61	1.18	89
Collectivist career tactics	3.11	3.46	2.84*	89
Hong Kong				
Individualistic career goals	4.07	3.86	1.54	66
Collectivist career tactics	3.41	3.34	.42	66
Singapore				
Individualistic career goals	3.96	3.94	.07	27
Collectivist career tactics	3.42	3.38	.17	27
Taiwan				
Individualistic career goals	3.88	3.36	3.13*	97
Collectivist career tactics	3.49	3.50	-.04	97

*$p < .05$.

career goals and tactics were associated with ethnicity and age. However, gender and firm type were not related to choices of career goals and tactics among the U.S. and Asian managers.

The U.S. managers are more likely to employ both individualistic and collectivist career tactics to achieve their career goals than Hong Kong and Singaporean managers. The Japanese managers do not consider collectivist career goals to be more important than the U.S. managers do, and the Japanese managers are not more likely to adopt collectivist career tactics to achieve their goals than the U.S. managers. There are several explanations for these findings. First, U.S. managers tend to be more action-oriented than Asians. Therefore, U.S. managers might be more likely to take different kinds of actions to reach their goals. Another possible explanation is that these findings may come from response biases. It is likely that U.S. respondents are prone to choose higher numbers when they respond to a Likert scale. The U.S. group would have higher means than the Japanese and Taiwanese managers on all scales. Another possible explanation is that the concept of "team" has been highly advocated in the U.S. recently. The U.S. managers are expected to express collaborative behavior in their workplaces. Hence, they will evaluate collectivist career goals as more important and consider it more likely to adopt collectivist career tactics that they would achieve their goals.

Finally, research has indicated that Japanese corporations today are less likely to provide lifetime employment to their employees than in the past (Pucik, 1984; Sethi, Namiki, & Swanson, 1984). As a result, employees may start to have a higher commitment to themselves than to their corporations. In order to remain employed in their current corporations, they will be more likely to pursue individual performance goals than they may have been in the past.

The common belief that female managers are more collectivist than male managers is not supported by this research. This study indicates that male and female managers do not value individualistic and collectivist career goals differently and they do not choose different career tactics to achieve their career goals. In fact, U.S. female managers, Hong Kong female managers, and Taiwanese female managers working for U.S. firms have higher means on individualistic career goals and tactics than do their male counterparts. One possible explanation for this phenomenon is that in order to be promoted to managerial positions, female managers in these countries are expected to express individualism outwardly. Another possibility is that individualistic female managers are more likely to be promoted to managerial positions in these countries.

The expectation that younger generations in Asian communities are more likely to choose individualistic career goals and tactics than older generations because of higher industrialization and more exposure to Western cultures is not fully supported by this study. This difference is found only in the Taiwanese and Japanese groups. A possible explanation for this finding is that both Hong Kong and Singapore were colonies of Western countries. Therefore, people in these countries have been exposed to individualistic cultural values for a long time. So there may be fewer differences between younger managers and older managers in the degree of individualism in Hong Kong and Singapore.

When the age effect was tested, the results indicated that there is a significant difference among managers in these Asian countries. Results indicate that it is not appropriate for multinational corporations to consider all Asian countries as a group when they manage career plans for their Asian employees from different countries. From Hofstede's (1980) study, Hong Kong, Japan, Taiwan, and Singapore are similar on three of the four universal culture values: power distance, individualism–collectivism, and masculinity. However, Japan has a higher score on uncertainty avoidance than other Chinese-majority countries. Future research can study how these cultural values interact to influence managers to select different career goals and tactics.

There are several limitations of this study. First, this study used a secondary data set to examine the hypotheses. When the individualistic and collectivist career goals and tactics scales were constructed, the selection of items was restricted to the existing questions asked by the previous researchers. Therefore, it is possible that the scales constructed in this study do not completely represent the concepts of individualistic career goals, collectivist career goals, individualistic career tactics, and collectivist career tactics. There is a need to construct standardized measurements of these concepts in future research.

Second, the results of the factor analysis show that when the U.S. data set, Japanese data set, and Chinese data set were analyzed separately, different items were included in the individualistic career tactics scales and the collectivist career tactics scales for these groups. For the individualistic career tactics scale, do something important that others will notice and do better than your peers were not included in the Chinese group, and create a job in your organization and gain more control were not contained in the Japanese group. For the collectivist career tactics scale, change your family plans to better fit your job was not included when data from different countries were analyzed separately. U.S. managers did not consider conform to what is expected a collectivist career tactic.

Because many researchers mention that individualism–collectivism is a multidimensional cultural value, there is a possibility that the scales constructed in this study present only a certain dimension of individualism–collectivism. Therefore, even though these items theoretically represent the definition of individualism–collectivism, they were left out from certain groups in this study. Alternatively, perhaps these constructs have slightly different meanings among U.S. managers and Asian managers. A future study designed to analyze differences in the meanings could illuminate these findings further.

Finally, the sample from each country is small, especially the Singaporean group (twenty-nine respondents). Small sample size can affect the statistical power of the study. It is possible that the nonsignificant effect between male and female managers is due to the small sample size of female managers. Hence, it is necessary to repeat these analyses with a larger sample to confirm this study's findings.

Overall, the findings of this study show some evidence that there are differences among U.S. and Asian managers in selection of career goals and tactics. However, several areas need to be clarified. First, some effort should be put into constructing better measures of individualistic career goals, collectivist career goals, individualistic career tactics, and collectivist career tactics. There is a need to clarify whether U.S. managers are more collectivist than they used to be or the findings are due to the effect of some response bias. Furthermore, the sample used in this study only includes managers. It would be interesting to examine whether similar results can be found in different levels of workers.

Multinational organizations may need to consider different career policies and paths for workers with different cultural backgrounds. Although several expected results were not found, the finding that Asian managers may be less proactive in all types of individualistic career tactics indicates that firms may need to take more initiative in assisting Asian employees in achieving their career goals.

REFERENCES

Aryee, S., & Debrah, Y. A. (1993). A cross-cultural application of a career planning model. *Journal of Organizational Behavior, 14*, 119–127.

Bartol, K. M. (1976). Relationship of sex and professional training area to job orientation. *Journal of Applied Psychology, 61*, 368–370.

Beres, M. E., & Portwood, J. D. (1981). Sociocultural influences on organizations: analysis of recent research. In G. W. England, A. R. Negandhi, & B. Wilpert (Eds.), *Functioning of Complex Organizations* (pp. 303–336). Cambridge, MA: Oelgeschlager, Gunn and Hain.

Burke, R. J. (1991). Organizational treatment of minority managers and professionals: Costs to the majority. *Psychological Reports, 68*, 439–449.

Child, J. D. (1981). Culture, contingency, and capitalism in the cross-national study of organization. In L. L. Cummings & G. M. Staw (Eds.), *Research in organizational behavior.* Greenwich, CT: JAI Publishers.

Chinese Culture Connection. (1987). Chinese values and the search for culture-free dimensions of culture. *Journal of Cross-Cultural Psychology, 18*(2), 143–164.

Eagly, A. H. (1987). *Sex differences in social behavior: A social-role interpretation.* Hillsdale, NJ: Erlbaum.

Falbo, T. (1977). Multidimensional scaling of power strategies. *Journal of Personality and Social Psychology, 35*, 537–547.

Gire, J. T., & Carment, D. W. (1983). Dealing with disputes: The influence of individualism–collectivism. *Journal of Social Psychology, 133*(1), 81–95.

Gould, S. (1979). Characteristics of planners in upwardly mobile occupations. *Academy of Management Journal, 22*, 539–550.

Granrose, C. S., & Portwood, J. (1987). Matching individual career plans and organizational career management. *Academy of Management Journal, 30*(4), 699–720.

Hall, D. T. (1971). A theoretical model of career subidentity development in organizational settings. *Organizational Behavior and Human Performance, 6*, 50–76.

Hicks, G. L., & Redding, S. G. (1983). The story of the East Asian "economic miracle": Part one, economic theory be damned. *Euro-Asia Business Review, 2*, 24–32.

Hofheinz, R., & Calder, K. E. (1982). *The East Asia edge.* New York: Basic Books.

Hofstede, G. (1980). *Culture's consequences.* Beverly Hills, CA: Sage.

Hofstede, G., & Bond, M. (1984). Hofstede's culture dimensions: An independent validation using Rokeach's value survey. *Journal of Cross-Cultural Psychology, 15*, 417–433.

Hui, C. H. (1988). Measurement of individualism–collectivism. *Journal of Research on Personality, 22*, 17–36.

Kahn, H., & Pepper, T. (1979). *The Japanese challenge: The success and failure of economic success.* New York: Thomas Y. Crowell.

Kipnis, D., Schmidt, S., & Wilkinson, I. (1980). Intraorganizational influence tactics: Explorations in getting one's way. *Journal of Applied Psychology, 65*, 440–452.

Knight, G. P., & Dubro, A. F. (1984). Cooperative, competitive, and individualistic social values: An individualized regression and clustering approach. *Journal of Personality and Social Psychology, 46*(1), 98–105.

Lykes, M. B. (1985). Gender and individualistic vs. collectivist bases for notions about the self. Special issue: Conceptualizing gender in personality theory and research. *Journal of Personality, 53*(2), 356–383.

Manhardt, P. J. (1972). Job orientation of male and female college graduates in business. *Personnel Psychology, 25*, 361–368.

McClelland, D. C., Atkinson, J. W., Russel, A. C., & Lowell, E. L. (1958). A scoring manual for the achievement motive. In J. W. Atkinson (Ed.), *Motives in fantasy, action, and society* (pp. 179–204). Princeton, NJ: Van Nostrand.

Meindl, J. R., Hunt, R. G., & Lee, W. (1989). Individualism-collectivism and work values: Data from the United States, China, Taiwan, Korea, and Hong Kong. *Research in Personnel and Human Resources Management, 1*, 59–77.

Meindl, J. R., Hunt, R. G., Lee, W. S., & Elizur, D. (1986). Work values and achievement orientations: Comparing the U.S.A. and China. *HRMOB Proceedings, 2*, 28–32.

MOW International Research Team. (1987). *The meaning of work.* New York: Academic Press.

Pucik, V. (1984). White-collar human resource management in large Japanese manufacturing firms. *Human Resource Management, 23*, 257–276.

Redding, S. G. (1990). *The spirit of Chinese capitalism.* New York: Walter de Gruyter.

Ronen, S. (1986). *Comparative and multinational management.* New York: Wiley.

Schwartz, S., & Bilsky, W. (1987). Toward a universal psychological structure of human values. *Journal of Personality and Social Psychology, 53*, 550–562.

Sethi, S. P., Namiki, N., & Swanson, C. L. (1984). The decline of the Japanese system of management. *California Management Review, 26*, 35–45.

Shenkar, O., & Ronen, S. (1987). Structure and importance of work goals among managers in the People's Republic of China. *Academy of Management Journal, 30*(3), 564–576.

Triandis, H. C. (1980). Values, attitudes, and interpersonal behavior. In H. Howe & M. Page (Eds.), *Nebraska Symposium on Motivation* (pp. 195–295). Lincoln: University of Nebraska Press.

Triandis, H. C. (1989). Cross-cultural studies of individualism and collectivism. In J. J. Berman (Ed.), *Nebraska symposium on motivation* (pp. 41–133). Lincoln: University of Nebraska Press.

Triandis, H. C., Bontempo, R., Villareal, M., Asai, M., & Lucca, N. (1988). Individualism-collectivism: Cross-cultural perspectives on self-ingroup relationships. *Journal of Personality and Social Psychology, 54*,(2) 323–338.

Triandis, H. C., Leung, K., Villareal, M. J., & Clark, F. I. (1985). Allocentric vs. idiocentric tendencies: Convergent and discriminant validation. *Journal of Research in Personality, 19*, 395–415.

Triandis, H. C., McCusker, C., & Hui, C. H. (1990). Multimethod probes of individualism and collectivism. *Journal of Personality and Social Psychology, 59*(5), 1006–1020.

Waterman, A. S. (1984). *The psychology of individualism*. New York: Praeger.

Wheeler, L., Reis, H. T., & Bond, M. H. (1989). Collectivism–individualism in everyday social life: The middle kingdom and the melting pot. *Journal of Personality and Social Psychology, 57*(1), 79–86.

Yamaguchi, S. (1994). Collectivism among the Japanese: A perspective from the self. In U. Kim, H. C. Triandis, C. Kagitcibasi, S. Choi, & G. Yoon (Eds.), *Individualism and collectivism* (pp. 175–188). Beverly Hills, CA: Sage.

Yu, A. -B., & Yang, K. -S. (1994). The nature of achievement motivation in collectivist societies. In U. Kim, H. C. Triandis, C. Kagitcibasi, S. Choi, & G. Yoon (Eds.), *Individualism and collectivism* (pp. 239–250). Beverly Hills, CA: Sage.

Interview Protocol for Line Managers: International Careers Project

This project seeks to identify the way managers from different countries think about the series of jobs they have held during their work life; that is, their *careers*. The research is sponsored by the U.S. Fulbright Research Grant program of the Council for International Exchange of Scholars, and by several universities. It is independent of your employer.

Responses of many managers working for different employers in different countries will be combined and reported to other scholars and to participating employers, but your individual responses will not be able to be identified in these summaries.

YOUR SPECIFIC ANSWERS WILL NEVER BE IDENTIFIED TO ANYONE OUTSIDE THE RESEARCH STAFF.

There are no correct answers to this questionnaire, nor is there one best way to think about your work as it extends through your life, so please tell us your personal opinion.

Please answer each question carefully and completely. We need answers to every page to be able to use your response fully. If a question or a response category is not applicable or not relevant for you, you can indicate this by writing NA beside the question, or by writing an explanation in the margin of the page.

In most cases there will be a question followed by a series of numbers. Circle the one number which most closely matches your opinion. In other cases there will be a blank space. Write your answer in the space provided.

Thank you for your willingness to cooperate with us in this important study. The results will help managers, companies, and students to better understand careers in the future.

Cherlyn S. Granrose, Ph.D., *Project Coordinator*
Temple University, Philadelphia, PA 19122 USA

Your Name :

Your Company*:

Today's Date:

Your Location: City: Country:

*In this questionnaire, "company" or "co." refers to your employer organization in one coun-
try or geographical region; the word "organization" refers to this company as well as any larger
parent organization that may operate in many countries.

CAREER PLANS

1. When you think about the very first occupation or real job you had after
   school, what was that job?

   What influenced your being in that job or occupation rather than another
   one? (family, school, friends, the job market, etc.)?

   At that time, what was your aspiration or career goal, if any?

2. If your occupation has changed or your career has had major shifts, how has
   it changed, and why? (For example, an occupational change might be from
   an engineer to a manager.)

   I changed from _____ to _____

   because

   I changed from _____ to _____

   because

3. If you had the chance to start your work life over again, would you choose

1	2
The Same Occupation	**A Different Occupation**

   Why?

4. How much have you thought about your career before answering this questionnaire?

1	2	3	4	5
Not at All				**A Great Deal**

5. Some people have very specific plans for their future and others do not. How
   specific are your plans for your future work life . . . your career plans?

1	2	3	4	5
I Have No Plans		**Very Specific**		**Very General**

6. How far into the future do you have plans for your career?

1	2	3	4	5
Day by Day	**1 Year**	**2-5 Years**	**6-10 Years**	**10+ Years**

7. Briefly describe any plans you have for your career.

8. Now, when you think about what you want from your work life or career, how would you define career success for yourself?

   How likely are you to achieve this success in your career?

1	2	3	4	5
0–20% Chance	**20–40%**	**40–60%**	**60–80%**	**80–100% Chance**

9. What, if anything, are you doing to have the kind of a work life or career you want? That is, do you have any career tactics?

10. What (or who) is most likely to prevent you or block you from having the career you want? Why will this be a block?

11. What (or who) is most likely to help you have the career you want? Why will this be a help?

12. In general, how do you feel about your career so far?

13. How do you combine your work and your personal (family or leisure) life (e.g., timing your marriage or children, separating work time and nonwork time.)?

14. People work for many different reasons, which we could call long-term career goals. Thinking about all of the jobs you will have in your work life, how important is it that your work life contains each of the following? (Circle one number for each item; ignore the column labeled RANK for now.)

Rank Career Goals	Of Little Importance		Moderately Important		Extremely Important
____ A good income	1	2	3	4	5
____ Esteem or prestige	1	2	3	4	5
____ Power and influence	1	2	3	4	5
____ Use of your skills & education	1	2	3	4	5
____ Creativity	1	2	3	4	5
____ Fun or enjoyment	1	2	3	4	5
____ Convenient working hours	1	2	3	4	5
____ Good relationships/friendship	1	2	3	4	5

Rank Career Goals	Of Little Importance		Moderately Important		Extremely Important
____ Advancement or promotions	1	2	3	4	5
____ Variety	1	2	3	4	5
____ Independence or autonomy	1	2	3	4	5
____ Achievement of challenges	1	2	3	4	5
____ Living where you want to	1	2	3	4	5
____ Contributing to your company	1	2	3	4	5
____ Contributing to your society	1	2	3	4	5
____ Contributing to your family	1	2	3	4	5
____ Job security, keeping your job	1	2	3	4	5
____ Comfortable working conditions	1	2	3	4	5
____ Keeping busy	1	2	3	4	5
____ Fringe Benefits	1	2	3	4	5
____ Meaningful or interesting work	1	2	3	4	5
____ Growth or learning new things	1	2	3	4	5
____ General well being	1	2	3	4	5

15. Now, please look back over this list and pick your top 5 career goals and rank order them. Write a 1 on the line in front of the most important one, a 2 in front of the next most important one, and so on, until you have ranked 5 goals.

16. People sometimes have short-term goals as well as long-term ones. Look at the list one more time and select the one thing that would influence you to change to a new job right now if you could change jobs now. Write that term here:

17. Thinking about all of your long term career goals, what do you expect to get out of working for your current organization?

0	1	2	3
I Have No Goals	It Is Not Related To My Goals	It Is a Path Toward My Goals	I Can Meet My Goals in This Org.

18. In general, how easy would it be for you to change from your job to another equal or better job in this organization, if you wanted to?

1	2	3	4	5
Almost Impossible				Very Easy

Why is this so?

19. In general, how easy would it be for you to obtain an equal or better job in a different organization, if you wanted to?

1	2	3	4	5
Almost Impossible				**Very Easy**

Why is this so?

20. In general, how satisfied are you with meeting your career goals so far in your life?

1	2	3	4	5
Very Dissatisfied				**Very Satisfied**

21. Overall, to what extent have your career expectations been met so far in your life?

1	2	3	4	5
Not at All Met My Expectations		**Just Met My Expectations**		**Greatly Exceeded My Expectations**

22. In general, how satisfied are you with your life?

1	2	3	4	5
Very Dissatisfied				**Very Satisfied**

23. How important and significant is working in your total life?

1	2	3	4	5
One of the Least Important Things				**One of the Most Important Things**

24. How much does work contribute to the way you feel about yourself?

1	2	3	4	5
Very Little				**Very Much**

25. How much has work influenced the kind of person you are?

1	2	3	4	5
Very Little				**Very Much**

CAREER STRATEGIES

26. In order to reach your career goals or have the kind of work life you want, how likely are you to do each of the following things? (Please circle one number per item; ignore RANK for now.)

Rank Strategies	Very Unlikely			Extremely Likely	
___ Work hard, give extra effort	1	2	3	4	5
___ Work long hours	1	2	3	4	5

Rank Strategies	Very Unlikely				Extremely Likely
____ Do your current job well	1	2	3	4	5
____ Do something important that others will notice	1	2	3	4	5
____ Do what your boss wants you to	1	2	3	4	5
____ Act humble or courteous toward your superiors	1	2	3	4	5
____ Assertively ask for what you want	1	2	3	4	5
____ Exchange favors with others	1	2	3	4	5
____ Threaten to leave or use other threats	1	2	3	4	5
____ Ask someone higher up or more powerful to help you	1	2	3	4	5
____ Develop an action plan to justify your choice	1	2	3	4	5
____ Seek help from your co-workers or friends	1	2	3	4	5
____ Show loyalty to your organization	1	2	3	4	5
____ Show loyalty to your superior	1	2	3	4	5
____ Learn more about the business	1	2	3	4	5
____ Get more education or training	1	2	3	4	5
____ Gain rapport with subordinates	1	2	3	4	5
____ Do better than your peers	1	2	3	4	5
____ Become indispensable	1	2	3	4	5
____ Gain access to important information	1	2	3	4	5
____ Conform to what is expected	1	2	3	4	5
____ Seek help from parents, spouse, or other family	1	2	3	4	5
____ Seek help from God, religious priests, or fortune teller	1	2	3	4	5
____ Change your family plans to better fit your job	1	2	3	4	5

Rank Strategies	Very Unlikely			Extremely Likely	
_____ Get a transfer to a different job in the same organization	1	2	3	4	5
_____ Get a job in a different organization	1	2	3	4	5
_____ Get a second job in addition to your present job	1	2	3	4	5
_____ Create a new job in the organization	1	2	3	4	5
_____ Seek more control over your present job	1	2	3	4	5
_____ Change the way you think about your job	1	2	3	4	5
_____ Build a network of contacts	1	2	3	4	5
_____ Start your own company	1	2	3	4	5
_____ Count on others to recognize your contribution	1	2	3	4	5
_____ Leave it to fate or others to decide	1	2	3	4	5
_____ Tell your boss your career plans	1	2	3	4	5
_____ Seek career guidance	1	2	3	4	5

27. Now, please look back over both pages and pick your 5 top strategies and rank them. Write a 1 on the line in front of your favorite strategy, a 2 in front of your next favored strategy, and so on, until you have marked 5 strategies. Do not forget to use both pages of alternative strategies for this question.

28. If you could change to another job either inside or outside of your organization, how much influence or control would each of the following have over which job you have as your next job? (If you do not think you will have another job in your life, use your present job as an example. Circle one number per item; ignore RANK for now.)

Rank	Very Little Influence			Very Much Influence	
_____ Number of available jobs	1	2	3	4	5
_____ The characteristics of the job	1	2	3	4	5
_____ The location of the job	1	2	3	4	5
_____ The future potential of the job	1	2	3	4	5

Rank	Very Little Influence				Very Much Influence
____ The company policies or personnel practices	1	2	3	4	5
____ The company reputation or image	1	2	3	4	5
____ The company's growth potential	1	2	3	4	5
____ The company's nationality	1	2	3	4	5
____ Your spouse	1	2	3	4	5
____ Your children	1	2	3	4	5
____ Your teacher	1	2	3	4	5
____ Your immediate superior	1	2	3	4	5
____ Your parents	1	2	3	4	5
____ Your friends and co-workers	1	2	3	4	5
____ Your spiritual priest or fortune teller	1	2	3	4	5
____ Government policy or laws	1	2	3	4	5
____ Political events	1	2	3	4	5
____ Community leaders	1	2	3	4	5
____ The school you graduated from	1	2	3	4	5
____ Your ethnic or regional origin	1	2	3	4	5
____ Your gender	1	2	3	4	5
____ Your social status	1	2	3	4	5
____ Grades or examination scores	1	2	3	4	5
____ Your skills or performance	1	2	3	4	5
____ Your seniority or tenure	1	2	3	4	5
____ Your values or beliefs	1	2	3	4	5
____ Your previous job experience	1	2	3	4	5
____ Your career plans	1	2	3	4	5
____ Your degree or certificates	1	2	3	4	5

29. Now, please look back over the list and select the 5 things that would most influence which job you have as your next job and rank them. Write a 1 on the line in front of the most influential, a 2 in front of the next most influential, and so on, until you have ranked the top 5.

ORGANIZATIONAL INFORMATION

The next part of this questionnaire asks about career management in your organization. Please give us your personal opinion of what your organization does. If something is not relevant for your company, but does happen in some other part of the larger organization, you may make a note of this in the margin.

30. How much of each of the following does this organization do to try to influence you to meet THEIR objectives FOR YOU in this organization?

	Very Little			Very Much	
Uses company songs or slogans to develop loyalty	1	2	3	4	5
Pays well	1	2	3	4	5
Gives good fringe benefits	1	2	3	4	5
Provides good working conditions	1	2	3	4	5
Gives employees influence in important decisions	1	2	3	4	5
Indirectly threatens to punish you or withhold rewards for nonconformity	1	2	3	4	5
Promotes teamwork	1	2	3	4	5
Gives rational arguments for why it is a good place to work	1	2	3	4	5
Appeals to nationalism	1	2	3	4	5
Offers appreciation	1	2	3	4	5
Uses authority based on family connections or status	1	2	3	4	5
States it is better than other competing organizations	1	2	3	4	5
Shares information about the co. and the role of employees in meeting co. goals	1	2	3	4	5
Offers broader job experience	1	2	3	4	5
Offers good career opportunities for the future	1	2	3	4	5
Offers good career training	1	2	3	4	5
Refers to the management culture or organizational mission	1	2	3	4	5
Treats you as a family member	1	2	3	4	5
Sets performance goals and rewards those who meet them	1	2	3	4	5

31. How satisfied are you that this organization provides you with each of the following opportunities or rewards? (Circle one number for each item. Note the direction of the scale.)

	Very Satisfied				Very Dissatisfied
A good income	1	2	3	4	5
Esteem or prestige	1	2	3	4	5
Power and influence	1	2	3	4	5
Use of your skills & education	1	2	3	4	5
Creativity	1	2	3	4	5
Fun or enjoyment	1	2	3	4	5
Convenient working hours	1	2	3	4	5
Good relationships/friendship	1	2	3	4	5
Advancement or promotions	1	2	3	4	5
Variety	1	2	3	4	5
Independence or autonomy	1	2	3	4	5
Achievement of challenges	1	2	3	4	5
Living where you want to	1	2	3	4	5
Contributing to your company	1	2	3	4	5
Contributing to your society	1	2	3	4	5
Contributing to your family	1	2	3	4	5
Job security	1	2	3	4	5
Comfortable working conditions	1	2	3	4	5
Keeping busy	1	2	3	4	5
Fringe benefits	1	2	3	4	5
Meaningful or interesting work	1	2	3	4	5
Growth or learning new things	1	2	3	4	5
General well being	1	2	3	4	5

32. How likely are each of the following to occur in this organization?

	Very Satisfied				Very Dissatisfied
Your organization has career plans for you	1	2	3	4	5
You know what your organization plans for your future	1	2	3	4	5

	Very Satisfied				Very Dissatisfied
Your career goals match your organization's goals for you	1	2	3	4	5
Your career timetable matches your organization's timetable for you	1	2	3	4	5
You can meet your career timetable in this organization	1	2	3	4	5
Your career strategy matches the organization's career strategy for your future	1	2	3	4	5
You can use your career strategy in this organization	1	2	3	4	5

33. Which of the following career management activities are available to you?

	Don't Know	Not Available	Available Informally	Available Formally
Posting of job openings (e.g., bulletin boards)	0	1	2	3
Career information (e.g., career pamphlets)	0	1	2	3
Career counseling	0	1	2	3
Performance review	0	1	2	3
Career testing (e.g., skills or values)	0	1	2	3
Job or task rotation	0	1	2	3
Coaching or mentors	0	1	2	3
Career planning workshops	0	1	2	3
Leadership or skill training workshops	0	1	2	3
Job or org. information	0	1	2	3
Others _____	0	1	2	3

34. How do they fill most positions at your level in this organization?

1	2	3	4
External Hire	**Promotion**	**Transfer**	**All of These Ways**

35. What kind of formal Human Resource Planning process does this organization have ?

0	1	2	3
Don't Know	**None**	**Ineffective**	**Effective**

36. Are there career paths or patterns most people follow in this organization?

1	2	3
None	**Informal Paths**	**Formal Paths**

37. How long do managers usually stay in the same position?

38. What are the most common criteria for promotion?

   (If it is good performance, what is considered good performance?)

   What are the criteria for lateral transfer?

39. Who decides who should be promoted?

CAREER HISTORY

If you have a resume that lists all your job experiences, you may want to use it to complete this page.

Please list, in order, all of the jobs you have held for six or more months. Begin with the first job you had where you worked at least 20 hours per week, and end with your current job. If there were times when you were not working for more than 6 months, record "Unemployed," the length of time, and the reason, such as school, child care, no job.

In the first column, record the nationality of the home office of the organization, the size of the organization, and the reason you joined and the reason you left that organization.

   Small = < 500 employees,

   Large = > 500 employees operating in one country,

   MNC = Multinational corporation

In the second column, record all of the positions you held in that organization.

In the third column record the approximate time you held each position.

In the last column, record whether each job was a step down (-), a lateral transfer (.), an expansion of your job duties (<), a promotion (+), or a change in title only (t).

Even though this page may be difficult, it is one of the most important pages in the questionnaire and we appreciate the extra effort you make to do this carefully.

You may continue onto the next page if you need the space. If you need more space for one organization, just change the numbers in the left margin.

Organization Nationality	Size S/L/MNC	Positions	Duration in Years	Mobility − . < + t

1. Joined because:

   Left because:

2. Joined because:

   Left because:

3. Reason for joining:

   Reason for leaving:

4. Reason for joining:

   Reason for leaving:

5. Reason for joining:

   Reason for leaving:

6. Reason for joining:

   Reason for leaving:

7. Reason for joining:

   Reason for leaving:

COMMITMENT

This part of the questionnaire asks about how important different aspects of your life are to you personally. Think of your current job in your current organization when answering these questions.

40. When you think about yourself, how important is it to see yourself as each of the following? (Circle one number per item.)

	Not Very Important			Very Important	
As a unique individual	1	2	3	4	5
As a member of your organization	1	2	3	4	5
As a member of your occupation or profession	1	2	3	4	5
As a resident or your community	1	2	3	4	5
As a member of your race or ethnic group	1	2	3	4	5
As a citizen of your country	1	2	3	4	5
As a citizen of the world	1	2	3	4	5

41. How much do you agree with each of the following statements?

	Strongly Disagree			Strongly Agree	
This organization means a lot to me	1	2	3	4	5
I live, eat, and breathe my job	1	2	3	4	5
I wish I had chosen a different occupation	1	2	3	4	5
I'm NOT part of this organizational family	1	2	3	4	5
The most important things in my life involve my job	1	2	3	4	5
I do NOT belong to this organization	1	2	3	4	5
My occupation reflects my personality	1	2	3	4	5
My job is only a small part of me	1	2	3	4	5
I want a career in my occupation	1	2	3	4	5
I am NOT motivated to work hard	1	2	3	4	5

	Strongly Disagree				Strongly Agree
My boss considers me an effective worker	1	2	3	4	5
If I work hard I will get rewarded	1	2	3	4	5
My job performance is poor	1	2	3	4	5
I am willing to do extra work to get the job done	1	2	3	4	5
My job performance is excellent	1	2	3	4	5

INDIVIDUAL INFORMATION

42. What is your gender?

1	2
Male	**Female**

43. What is your marital status?

1	2	3	4
Single	**Married**	**Divorced/Separated**	**Widowed**

44. If married, what is the occupation of your spouse?

    (If your spouse is now a homemaker, but was employed, what was that occupation?)

45. If your spouse is employed, how many hours a week does he or she work?

46. How many children do you have?   Age of youngest?

47. In all, how many people do you support, counting yourself?

48. What is your ethnic or racial group?

49. What is your nationality?

50. If your nationality is different from your passport, what passport do you hold?

51. What is your religious or philosophical background?

1	2	3	4	5	6	7
None	**Jewish**	**Catholic**	**Protestant**	**Muslim**	**Confucian**	**Taoist**
8	9	10	11	12	13	14
Buddhist	**Hindu**	**Sikh**	**Shinto**	**Janism**	**Parsi**	**Other**_____

52. What is the highest level of education you have completed?

1	2	3	4	5	6	7
Primary School	Junior High	High School	Jr. Tech College	Bachelor's Degree	Master's Degree	Ph.D.

53. If you attended college or university, what was your major in your final degree?

1	2	3
No College or University	Business	Math, Science, Engineering, Computers

4	5	6	7
Liberal Arts	Social Sciences	Fine Arts Humanities	Other _____

54. Did you graduate with honors?

1	2
No	Yes

55. Where did you grow up?

1	2	3
Country	Small Town	Large City

56. What kind of work did your father do?

57. Was your mother employed when you were a child?

1	2
No	Yes

If so, what did she do?

58. What is your primary language or dialect?

59. What other languages or dialects do you speak well enough to use at work?

60. In what year were you born?

61. How long do you expect to continue working for this organization?

62. How many hours per week do you actually work?

63. How willing would you be to accept a lateral transfer to another country if asked?

1	2	3	4	5
Extremely Unwilling				Extremely Willing

64. How willing would you be to accept a promotion that required you to move to another country?

1	2	3	4	5
Extremely Unwilling				**Extremely Willing**

65. How many management levels are there between you and the most senior person in this organization in this country?

66. What is your annual salary?

CAREER PATTERNS

67. Thinking of a career as all of the jobs you have held in your working life, extending across time, draw a picture to represent your career from its beginning to its end. For example, it may be a line which goes up or down or curves or spirals. It may also be a mixture of words and pictures. There is no correct way to draw this picture; just express yourself in your own way. Label in your picture the point or piece that represents the present.

Looking at the picture you have drawn, how would you describe to another person what it means to you? You can put labels on your picture to help you explain it.

JOB CHART CODE SHEET

40. How many years have you been working?

41. If you had been out of work for more than 6 months, why were you not working?

1	2	3	4
Couldn't Find a Job	**Child Care**	**School**	**Other**_____

42. How many different organizations have you worked for so far in your career?

44. What was the longest time you worked for one organization?

45. What was the shortest time you worked for one organization?

46. How many different positions have you held counting all organizations together?

47. How many significant promotions have you had in your career so far?

48. What was the longest time between promotions in your career?

49. What was the shortest time between promotions in your career?

50. How many demotions have you had?

51. How many lateral transfers to a job of equal status or responsibility have you had in your career so far?

52. How many times has the nature of the job expanded even though the job had the same position or job title?

53. How many different countries have you worked in?

54. Which countries?

55. How long have you held your current position?

56. How long have you worked for this organization?

Appendix B

Interview Protocol for Human Resources Managers: International Careers Project

This project seeks to identify the way managers from different countries think about the series of jobs they have during their work life, that is, their CAREERS. The research is sponsored by the U.S. Fulbright Research Grant program of the Council for International Exchange of Scholars and by several universities. It is independent of financial support of this organization; however, your organization has agreed to let its managers participate.

Responses of many organizations in many countries will be combined and reported to other scholars and to participating organizations, but your information will not be able to be identified in these summaries.

YOUR SPECIFIC ANSWERS WILL NEVER BE IDENTIFIED TO ANYONE OUTSIDE THE RESEARCH STAFF.

In order to understand the organizational context within which the managers of this organization think about their careers, it is important to understand its formal and informal policies and practices. Please answer each question carefully and completely. If a question or response category is not relevant for your organization, please be sure to explain what is relevant to your organization.

Thank you for your willingness to cooperate with us in this important study. The results will help managers, organizations, and scholars to better understand career management in the future.

Cherlyn S. Granrose, Ph.D.
Project Coordinator
Temple University
Philadelphia, PA 19122 USA

HR Manager's Name: Organization:

Date: Location:

Interviewer:

ORGANIZATIONAL STRUCTURE

The first part of this interview addresses the overall structure of the organization which shapes the kinds of careers that might be possible here.

1. Where is the location of the home office of this organization?

   If this is not the home office, what is the structural relationship between the organizational operations in this country and the home office (i.e., is this a subsidiary company, a joint venture, a regional office, a lessee, etc.)?

2. In which other countries does this organization operate?

   Parent Organization

   This Company

3. Which of these countries would it be possible for managers from this organization in this country to move into or out of?

   (Circle the country names above and write the total number here.)

4. What are the departments or parts of this organization that report to the most senior manager in this organization in this country? (Record the department names and the total number.)

   In your opinion, which are the most powerful departments in this list (i.e., the departments that can get what they want)?

   The least powerful?

5. How many levels of managers are there from the most senior to the least senior manager in this organization in this country?

   (Include as a manager anyone above foreman or manufacturing line supervisor who supervises two or more people or who has an equivalent position in the organization but does not have supervisory responsibilities because of technical responsibilities.)

   Would it be possible for me to have an organizational chart that shows the management of this organization in this country?

   If you have a mission statement or a copy of the organizational goals, any statements about your management philosophy or culture, and a copy of the latest annual report, I would like these also.

If these are not available, what would you say the mission or goals of this organization are?

The management philosophy?

HUMAN RESOURCES POLICY AND PRACTICE

6. Does this organization have a formal human resources planning process?

   If so, how does it work?

   Probe: How is it tied to human resources planning practices in the home office?

   Probe: How is it tied to strategic planning?

   Probe: Does it use an employee data bank?

   Is it computerized?

   Is it tied to other countries or the home office data bank?

   Would it be possible for me to get a demographic description of your managers, including age, sex, and nationality, from this data bank? (If not, would it be possible to the get total number of managerial and nonmanagerial employees?)

7. How do you usually get new potential managers?

   How many mangers will you hire this year?

   At what levels?

   How many will transfer in?

   At what levels?

   From where?

   What are the entry qualifications?

   Probe: which is more important, experience or educational certification?

8. Are there formal or informal career paths or patterns in this organization?

   If so, could you describe the most common alternative career paths for a manager moving from an entry-level position to an executive position in this organization.

   Probe: What is the most common first appointment?

   How long would he or she stay there?

   Then what would happen?

Next?

Next?

Next?

Next?

Probe: What would a person have to do to have this kind of a career path? (Seek informal rules.)

Anything else?

Probe: If there are formal paths, who knows these exist?

Probe: How might these career paths differ between a person from the country of the home office of this organization and a person from another country?

9. Are there any formal career management or career planning activities provided for managers to help them reach their career goals in this organization? If so, what are they and who is eligible?

   Show the list of Career Management Activities now and ask . . .

   Which of the following career management activities are available to managers in this organization in this country?

10. How long do managers usually stay in the same position?

11. What are the criteria for promotion?

   (If the criterion is good performance, what does this mean?)

12. What are the criteria for lateral transfer?

13. Who usually decides who should be considered for promotion or transfer?

14. At which points are managers most likely to leave this organization? What percent leave at each of these points?

   Why do you think they leave then?

15. What is your annual managerial turnover rate, approximately?

   Voluntary

   Involuntary

16. What are the most difficult human resources problems in this organization in this country?

17. What have you tried to do to solve these problems, and how successful have these attempts been?

18. How much does this organization use each of the following strategies to retain good employees or to encourage employees to have the careers it wants them to have? (Give the human resources strategies form.)

19. Is there anything else that I should know about this organization or its human resources policies or practices which would help me understand the careers of the managers here?

Thank you very much for your help. When we have tabulated all of the responses from all of the organizations, we would be happy to send you a summary of the results.

(Be sure you have a business card with a mailing address before you leave.)

CAREER MANAGEMENT ACTIVITIES

Which of the following career management activities are available to managers in this company? (Circle one number per item.)

	Not Available at All	Not Available in This Place	Available Informally	Available Formally
Posting of job openings	0	1	2	3
Career Information	0	1	2	3
Career Counseling	0	1	2	3
Performance Review	0	1	2	3
Career Testing	0	1	2	3
Job or task rotation	0	1	2	3
	Not Available at All	Not Available in This Place	Available Informally	Available Formally
Coaching or mentors	0	1	2	3
Career planning workshops	0	1	2	3
Leadership or skill training workshops	0	1	2	3
Job or organization information	0	1	2	3
Others _____	0	1	2	3

ORGANIZATIONAL RETENTION STRATEGIES

How much does this organization use each of the following strategies to try and retain good employees or to encourage employees to have the career it wants for them?

	Not Very Much			Very Much	
Uses company songs or slogans to develop loyalty	1	2	3	4	5
Pays well	1	2	3	4	5
Gives good fringe benefits	1	2	3	4	5
Gives good working conditions	1	2	3	4	5
Gives employees influence in important decisions	1	2	3	4	5
Indirectly threatens to punish or withhold rewards for nonconformity	1	2	3	4	5
Promotes teamwork	1	2	3	4	5
Gives rational arguments for why it is a good place to work	1	2	3	4	5
Appeals to nationalism	1	2	3	4	5
Offers appreciation	1	2	3	4	5
Uses authority based on family connections or status	1	2	3	4	5
States it is better than other competing organizations	1	2	3	4	5
Shares information about co. and role of employees in meeting co. goals	1	2	3	4	5
Offers broad job experience	1	2	3	4	5
Offers good career opportunities for the future	1	2	3	4	5
Offers good career training	1	2	3	4	5
Refers to management culture or organizational mission	1	2	3	4	5
Treats you as a family member	1	2	3	4	5
Sets performance goals and rewards those who meet them	1	2	3	4	5
Others _____	1	2	3	4	5

Index

About the Editor
and Contributors

MICHAEL B. ARTHUR is professor of management at the Sawyer School of Management, Suffolk University, Boston, Massachusetts. He holds his Ph.D. and M.B.A. degrees from Cranfield University, Warwick, United Kingdom. He is coeditor of *The Boundaryless Career: A New Employment Principle for a New Organizational Era* and *The Handbook of Career Theory*, and a coauthor of *Strategy Through People*.

MASAO BABA received his M.A. in industrial organizational psychology. Since 1970 he has been teaching industrial organizational psychology at the college of economics, Nihon University, Japan. He has authored *Organizational Behavior* and many other books in the field of industrial organizational psychology. He is a board member of the Japanese Association of I/O Psychology, as well as a member of the Academy of Management and the American Psychological Association. His areas of research are Japanese management systems and family systems and international career development. He is also trying to create a unified theory of organizational behavior.

ALLAN BIRD is professor of international management at the college of business, Polytechnic State University, in San Luis Obispo. His research focuses on aspects of Japanese executive careers—advancement, succession, compensation, and strategic change—as well as human resources management practices in Japanese overseas affiliates.

IRENE HAU-SIU CHOW is professor of management at the Chinese University of Hong Kong. She earned her B.B.A. degree from the Chinese University of Hong Kong and her M.B.A. and Ph.D. from Georgia State University. Her teaching and research interests focus on human resources management, Chinese business, and comparative business strategy. Her recent book is *Business Strategy: Asia Pacific Focus.*

CHERLYN SKROMME GRANROSE is professor of organizational behavior in the Claremont Graduate School, Claremont, California. She received her B.A. and M.A. degrees from the University of Michigan and her Ph.D. from Rutgers, the State University of New Jersey. She does career-related research in women's work/family issues, employee participation, and Asian human resources. She recently coauthored *Work-Family Role Choices for Women in Their 20s and 30s* and coedited *Cross Cultural Work Groups.*

REY-YEH LIN is a doctoral student in psychology in the Center for Organizational and Behavioral Science at Claremont Graduate School, Claremont, California, where she received her M.A. Her research interest includes career management issues in a cross-cultural context and human resources management.

TAI-KUANG PENG is professor of management at the Chinese Naval Academy, Kaohsiung, Republic of China. He received his Ph.D. from Texas Tech University. His current research interests focus on values and military socialization, as well as international human resources management issues. These issues include career concepts and career processes in East Asia.

ISBN 1-56720-101-6

HARDCOVER BAR CODE